T0012974

SPIRIT GUIDE INVOCATIONS

© Billie Topa Tate

About the Author

Billie Topa Tate is a third-generation Mescalero Apache medicine woman who mentored under her mother, grandmother, and elders. She is an active member of the American Indian Center in Chicago. She also owns and operates MSI Wellness Center where she offers mentoring, reiki, and energy sessions as well as teaching classes that help others find their own sacred journeys. Visit her at MSI-Healing.com.

SPIRIT GUIDE INVOCATIONS

Seeking Wisdom from Sacred Helpers

BILLIE TOPA TATE

Llewellyn Publications
Woodbury, Minnesota

Spirit Guide Invocations: Seeking Wisdom from Sacred Helpers Copyright © 2024 by Billie Topa Tate. All rights reserved. No part of this book may be used or reproduced in any manner whatsoever, including internet usage, without written permission from Llewellyn Worldwide Ltd., except in the case of brief quotations embodied in critical articles and reviews.

First Edition
First Printing, 2024

Book design by R. Brasington
Cover design by Kevin R. Brown
Editing by Marjorie Otto

Llewellyn Publications is a registered trademark of Llewellyn Worldwide Ltd.

Library of Congress Cataloging-in-Publication Data (Pending)
ISBN: 978-0-7387-7418-3

Llewellyn Worldwide Ltd. does not participate in, endorse, or have any authority or responsibility concerning private business transactions between our authors and the public.

All mail addressed to the author is forwarded but the publisher cannot, unless specifically instructed by the author, give out an address or phone number.

Any internet references contained in this work are current at publication time, but the publisher cannot guarantee that a specific location will continue to be maintained. Please refer to the publisher's website for links to authors' websites and other sources.

Llewellyn Publications
A Division of Llewellyn Worldwide Ltd.
2143 Wooddale Drive
Woodbury, MN 55125-2989
www.llewellyn.com

Printed in the United States of America

Acknowledgments

I dedicate this book, first, to my daughter Monique Little Doll. Her continuous wisdom, earnest efforts, great tenacity of spirit, joyful grace, and beautiful presence has been such a blessing to me since the time of her birth. Her great insights and wonderful assistance in developing this book is so much appreciated. Many thanks, Monique, for supplying your support and energy into the creation of this book. Da Go Tey.

To my husband, who supports my work. Neil has been my greatest advocate and my heart is filled with joy and great appreciation for all the work and efforts he has gifted me all these wonderful years. Many thanks, Neil; I am so grateful for your constant efforts to help and support all aspects of my work. I am deeply grateful. Thank you.

To my dear mother, Mama Little Wolf, my first teacher; to my father, Papa Little Wolf, my second teacher; to my sisters, brothers, nephews, and nieces: many blessings to you, and thank you.

I am in deep gratitude to my virtuous teachers, divine helpers, powerful ancestors, plant medicine teachers and plant medicine spirits, animal medicine spirits, my personal guides, and angels who have been with me to help me and guide me. I invoke for your divine presence in my life and within the lives of my family. Thank you, and please continue to surround me and my loved ones with your powerful energies.

To my wonderful teachers, who have guided me, taught me great things, and continue to mentor me and surround me with virtuous helpers from the spirit realm. Thank you.

To all my readers, please remember that you are the spirit of light walking on Mother Earth. May you always follow the integrity of your divine light and keep finding and seeking what inspires your great purpose. All good things to you.

Thank you with all my heart and spirit.

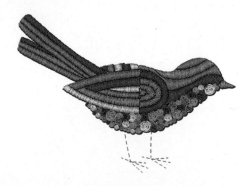

Contents

INTRODUCTION

This book is about ancient native wisdom that opens sacred space and time to connect with our virtuous spirit guides and angels. The reader of this book will receive information regarding energetic writings called *sacred invocations* that will provide wisdom-filled spirit support to help resolve stressful situations within any part of their lives.

I am a third-generation Mescalero Apache woman. This book begins with a rare glimpse into the world of the old ethereal wisdom of our Apache elders. My teachers taught me that words make worlds. Our native Apache elders shared priceless information regarding why and how to use medicine words as instructed by their celestial teachers, which were from the lands beyond the heavens.

Even though I am of Apache heritage, the story of my name, *Billie Topa Tate*, honors my Lakota teachers who blessed my name as a young woman. These teachers include Wallace Black Elk Jr. and the medicine woman Blue Star. I use this name in honor of them.

At Wallace Black Elk Jr.'s death bed, my mother and I sang a drumming song to honor him. He did a short song and said to me, "Wind that sings in the four directions is your name: Topa Tate." He transitioned to the spirit world soon after our visit. He was a good soul and great teacher to many on this beautiful Mother Earth.

My Apache name is private and only used by my family members because it's a sacred name. My Apache name means "Wind that Sings," which means I am here to share wisdom as my life's purpose. In part one of this book, I'll share my native teachings regarding the connection to the spirit world, the beings who are helping us in this work, and how invocations work. I will share the beauty of energetic narratives called *sacred invocations*. In part two, I'll share examples of invocations for specific situations to give you a starting place from which to build your own invocations. These invocations provide power via a string of words to petition the assistance of our energetic resources, called spirit guides and angels.

I have included my personal stories to help the reader gain more knowledge as to why our spirit guides help us. This book will also welcome the reader to receive the energy of our elders when reading each chapter, which equates to walking with a elder who shares the why of the universe as it pertains to each topic within each chapters.

I will introduce you to the concept of enlightened language used by my elders to engage and utilize energetic narratives, otherwise known as sacred invocations, to open windows of time to receive wisdom, healing energies, and transform the energy of difficult situations.

I was trained by Mama Little Wolf, my mother. I was also trained by my father, Papa Little Wolf, in addition to many teachers both inside and outside of our culture.

My mother and father graced the lands of the Southwest during their early lives to work the fields and develop a deeper relationship with the land. I was so very fortunate to live my younger life in the wellness of the natural world. The natural world is the doorway to our wellness and the doorway to the Great Spirit who created us.

During my later adolescent years, our family needed to settle into the city to secure higher paying jobs, but we kept to our wonderful wisdom practices and training.

Our spirit helpers come from the energy world of where the Creator maintains the Place of Light. Our energetic resources include our divine helpers, spirit guides, personal guides, specialized angels, the medicine spirits of the plants, the medicine spirit of the sacred water, the spirit totems, the holy medicine people, our virtuous ancestors and so many more. We were taught how to ask for their wisdom and help. This book will provide fresh new wisdom and ancient techniques on how to access this wonderful realm of help, healing, support, and divine intervention. My teachers spoke about ancient relationships with the Great Spirit, our spirit guides, the plant medicine spirits, and all the wonderful energy helpers within the realm of the spirit world that help us to understand our great purpose and our relationship with all the kingdoms on Mother Earth and with the Creator.

The first part of this book provides the ancient training of the medicine woman regarding the principles of the universe and how this information can help our daily lives and the daily lives of our loved ones.

The second part of this book consists of the actual written examples of sacred invocations to facilitate energy from the realm where our spirit guides, divine helpers, plant medicine spirits, and specialized angels reside. You'll be able to look up various situations that commonly happen in life and use the written invocation to help transform the energy and the situation. There are personal teachings that explain how I used these invocations and the universal principles of why they work.

The proof is in the actual experience of their help, as well as learning and understanding the universal principles of why they help us and the actual implementation of these wonderful sacred invocations. This is the first time many of these wisdom teachings will be seen by the public. However, I believe it is time to share this information in order for the world to experience peace, harmony, wisdom, and many other virtues. I am excited to share this information with you in hopes that you can clearly experience touching the light and see how energy can cross the span of time and space to help you.

Enjoy your journey into the world of the medicine woman, the realm of ancient and time-treasured knowledge, and implementation tools for your life's journey.

May you follow the integrity of your inner light.

How to Use This Book

This book welcomes you through chapters of written invocations, each of which guide you to resolve situations in your life that need healing energy and thus promote enlightenment, virtuous energy, wisdom, evolution, Sacred Balance, and happiness. These invocations can also help in the lives of others. The invocations are virtuous words wisely positioned within the energetic narrative. The language is called *enlightened language* in order to invoke and secure energetic assistance. Enlightened language was used by elders who conversed with our spirit helpers to receive wisdom and intervention. I've organized this book to contain within each invocation chapter a supporting personal story that helps deepen the understanding of the application of the invocation, followed by a written invocation that you can use to help your personal situation at any time.

There are two ways to utilize the book. You can use this book in a "cookbook" fashion, meaning you can look up a specific situation rather than read through the whole book. However, I suggest you read through the entire book, then use a chapter that will help you with a particular situation within your life. There are pearls of wisdom within each chapter that will help you to develop deeper wisdom on how to use the invocations. As you gain experience, you may feel comfortable not only utilizing the invocations within this book, but also writing your own invocations to handle specialized situations within your life.

I've selected a wide range of life situations designed to be used very much like a cookbook or instruction guide. Each chapter has supporting wisdom that will help you gain more expertise. You will also find short but helpful recommendations that encourage you to explore enrichment techniques for good self-care. These options are there to create more opportunities to work with your wonderful inner wisdom, spirit guides, and your personal virtuous teachers in spirit.

Now that you know a little about me, my native wisdom training, and how to use this book, enjoy and rediscover the profound ancient wisdom that is timeless and can be utilized within your daily life. The invocations are an opportunity to take in the great help of your spirit guides and spirit helpers, which is your birth right. Enjoy the journey.

Part 1

THE PRACTICE

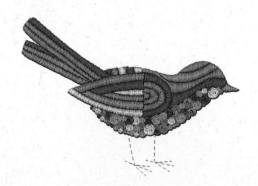

Chapter 1

ENERGETIC NARRATIVES CALLED SACRED INVOCATIONS

Energetic narratives are virtuous invocations that call on the assistance from our energetic resources. Energetic resources include spirit helpers, personal guardian angels, spirit guides, the archangels, virtuous teachers in spirit, divine helpers, spirit messengers, spirit totem helpers, our higher self, our family members on the other side, our companion animals on the other side, specialized inner plane helpers, and any other wonderful beings who assist us in virtuous ways.

The following chapters contain previously little-known information, philosophies, ancient wisdom, and instructions regarding the calling upon of our divine helpers for the purposes of providing energy, mentorship, healing, resolution, and intervention here on earth regarding stressful situations within our lives. Everything revolves around what your situation and your needs are, or rather, your stress points that need resolution and assistance.

A philosophy I often follow is the old saying "As above, so below." This means that depending upon what you need assistance with on our plane, divine helpers may enlist specialized divine helpers from higher planes to assist. Just as all humans can do many things and at times do them well, we often gravitate to specifics skills and have specialized areas of expertise and talents. As above so below, meaning our inner plane helpers and angels do many things and have their own special talents and strong suits.

Energy is the core medium of all things. My oral traditions share the ancient stories that speak about the elevated language of our virtuous mentors who shared with us energetic narratives that can be used to call upon them for help. This enlightened language creates a vibrational bridge to speak with divine helpers. These divine helpers have taught that our conversations and words with them need to have an elevated vibration in order to help us activate parts of our mind that can communicate with our divine helpers.

How to Use a Sacred Invocation

An invocation is used when help is needed from virtuous helpers, divine helpers, and our virtuous ancestors. When reading an invocation, it is important to focus on the invocation and read the invocation (if possible) out loud. Speaking out loud helps empower your intention and helps you focus on your request. Our mind has continuous thoughts, so many thoughts that our consciousness may have difficulty directing energy to specific situations that need help. However, when we use the power of words, we focus the energy of manifestation and thus, reading invocations out loud is very powerful. If you cannot read an invocation out loud, read it slowly in your internal voice with great intention and great respect and gratitude.

Read the invocation at night before you go to sleep, as this will help move the energy even more into the power aspect of dream time. If possible, read the invocation at least two to three times a day until the situation has been totally resolved and the stressful energy has been removed.

Use a journal to take notes from the streams of insight and wisdom that might come to you throughout the day. If you receive insight and inspiration advising you to adjust your invocation or add some additional information into your invocation, please do so. This type of information comes when your guides are helping you fine-tune your invocation narrative. Throughout the time you are reading your invocation, it is okay to fine-tune your narrative as needed. Your guides will be helping you to make small or large adjustments to help optimize your invocation to better serve the resolutions of your stressful situation. This will help you develop your skills for your current request and all other future requests. I recommend practicing meditation daily to help receive more virtuous guidance for a successful resolution of your situation or request.

The energetic word *secure* is very important within the invocations, as it helps divine helpers provide their expertise to any given situation. Also, the phrase *thank you* at the end of an invocation is important to let your spirit guides and divine helpers know that the invocation and request is completed.

Another helpful recommendation is to take time to read your invocation into a recording device, such as your smart phone. This will be helpful when you periodically come home tired and don't have the energy to read the invocation. Keeping your recorded invocation on your smart phone is very helpful throughout the day to apply more energy to resolving your situation. Take time to listen to your invocation at bedtime when you are too tired to read it out loud and, additionally, I would suggest listening to it midday, perhaps at lunch. This will help optimize the energy of resolving your situation.

An invocation needs to be read daily until the energy and the situation feels resolved and you receive a deep sense of wisdom and insight about the situation. When the profound insight or epiphany occurs, it will actually release the congested energy within your energy field regarding the situation and you will feel lighter and experience a quality of healing. Often, we learn so much about why the stressful situation occurred and some greater insight regarding all the people who were involved. You will notice that your feelings about the stressful situation you are working on will change into one or more of the virtues of peace, healing, and wisdom.

If you miss a day or even an entire week of reading an invocation, please start up again as soon as possible and continue until your situation has been resolved. The energy you may have placed previously into the invocation accumulates over time, so you will not have lost anything.

Keep in mind that whatever your situation is within the invocation, whether it is a trauma from the past, a pending situation that needs guidance, or something that needs assistance for the future, it is important to reflect on an important principle: Mother Earth is a place where we enjoy the world, but it is also a learning place. We are learning from every situation. We have great potential to evolve from every situation. What we learn from these situations is just as valuable as the actual event itself.

One of the fastest ways of receiving assistance is to include within your invocation that you would like to evolve and enlighten not only yourself, but everyone and everything that is involved within the invocation. This gives permission to divine helpers to cross the span of time and space to help in a deeper manner. These beings are not only helping us, but also helping everyone and everything involved to receive peace, wisdom, wholeness, and maturity. This is what the Great Spirit wants for everyone and everything.

Besides focusing on your current stressful situation, try to integrate into your invocation a pathway of genuine desire to serve. This may be in the form of some type of assistance that enhances the lives of any or all the kingdoms: the animal kingdom, the plant kingdom, and the human kingdom. This creates magical and healing outcomes.

How Invocations Work

The term *invoke* generally means to summon into action or bring into existence, often as if by magic. I define the word *invoke* as a powerful focused intention to connect with the more subtle energy realm where angels, divine helpers, virtuous teachers in spirit, totem helpers, plant spirit medicine, and personal guides reside. A sacred invocation is an energetic tool that was gifted to humans from the Great Spirit to materialize a platform by which wisdom and healing energies can be given to us.

The energy of time and the energy of words are divinely and uniquely intertwined. Energy, when focused upon, feels the quality of the focus and responds. This occurs at an atomic level. The element of time is also an interesting gift from the Creator, which allows for things to manifest in divine timing for our evolution. Teachers use the time platform to go back in time and to move into the future for healing and to gain wisdom.

Invocations are mystical narratives, and the powerful placement of words in these invocations guides energy to establish a connection with the realm of healing and divine helpers. An invocation is an energetic tool used by master teachers and virtuous mystics to encourage and navigate healing energy from the plant medicine world and the Place of Light. The Place of Light is also known as the world of angels, divine helpers, and our inner plane helpers. Invoking for their assistance carries the great potential of receiving help from our virtuous ancestors, holy medicine people, the plant spirit medicine world, our divine helpers, and even the archangels themselves.

The most insightful action performed by mystical teachers is using the energy language of an invocation to establish a fellowship and work with divine helpers to bring forth virtuous qualities of emotions for people to begin their healing process. An imbalance of emotions creates an imbalance within our relationships, especially the relationship we have with ourselves and the actions we take toward ourselves. Emotional blocks need to be released to achieve the healing of illness or the healing of a trauma. Often, the buildup of emotional energy produces physical situations and symptoms. An emotional impediment blocks the healthy flow of energy everywhere in the body. This makes one feel out of touch with people because they are out of touch with their own true virtuous qualities and feelings.

The Great Spirit gifted us the power of words, and when they are used in a medicine way (a healing way) they hold a tremendous amount of power. According to our native stories, divine helpers, angels, luminaries, archangels, plant spirit medicine, virtuous teachers in spirit, and all other virtuous inner plane helpers have within their energy field a commitment to the Great Spirit to provide assistance to all the kingdoms on Mother Earth, especially the human kingdom. The goal of this commitment to the Great Spirit is to bring about evolution by supplying the qualities of virtuous wisdom, healing energy, and intervention when called upon. Thus, the angels and other helpers can cross the span of vibrations and worlds to assist us.

One of the policies of the Great Spirit is to bring all events— past, present, and future—to their highest vibrational state. All the divine helpers know this, as it is their job to help with this process. The invocations within this book are the doorways into this world for these beings to help us.

Many years ago, my teacher told me that Mother Earth is a learning place, a coveted plane. This means that whatever we brought from other lifetimes to this lifetime will need to be worked out here in this lifetime. My teacher also told me that when you are in the energy world, if you don't like where you are or what is happening to you, you can think yourself somewhere else. However, that would mean that nothing would get resolved or accomplished. But on earth, in our physical bodies, when we are experiencing a problem or we are dealing with a stressful situation, we can't think ourselves somewhere else; we must work it out. This is a very good thing, as there is progress for resolution and we mature and grow from that experience. We focus on the situation that needs to be resolved, thus wisdom comes to us. This is what my teacher meant when he said this lifetime of walking on Mother Earth is a coveted lifetime. Energy tools, such as the energetic writings within this book, help to receive assistance in this lifetime.

Here is an interesting story about one of my teachers regarding how to use the energetic tool of time via a sacred invocation. My teacher agreed to find his way back to a campsite without any navigation tools after being driven far away into the mountains. As he stepped out of the vehicle, he did a quiet sacred invocation. He did not have a map nor any locating devices, only water. He began to run along the trails of the mountains. He appeared to be moving as if he was in a hurry and in a most confident manner. Soon he approached the camp and was welcomed by the person who drove him to the location. The driver asked, "How did you do this? How did you find your way back to the camp?" My teacher smiled and said, "I simply used a sacred invocation to go back to a time when you were jogging and walking briskly back to the camp and I then simply ran alongside you all the way here." This is a great demonstration of how a teacher can use the power of an invocation to wisely navigate time and step into another realm to use it for something that is needed in this realm.

Most people would not think to use an invocation to invoke such information. The majority of people solely use time to move forward in their daily lives, such as to go to work, go to the store, or to plan out the week. However, a very wise teacher knows that energy crosses the span of time and space to access very knowledgeable information.

May this book and all our wonderful divine helpers surround you and your loved ones with the qualities of peace, joy, good health, and, most of all, virtuous wisdom. Enjoy this mystical book and please share with others.

Chapter 2

WHY ANGELS AND
SPIRIT GUIDES HELP US

In the realm of the universe as well as our own personal energy field, there is the existence of a seed of pure light. This seed of pure light contains the Creator's great purpose, a sort of alchemic energy imprint. All sentient beings have this light. Even fallen angels have this light, but they are not using it. Fallen angels are often called *lesser lights*.

How do the angels and spirit guides help us, especially when working with all the sacred invocations within this book? The sacred invocations within this book are written carefully. Elders positioned meaningful words within these sacred invocations that would carry energy to fortify particles of spirit and light for our petitions for help and assistance. These particles of energy extend and build a landscape of spirit energy that summons and invokes angels and spirit helpers from the realm of light. These spirit helpers travel across the span of time and space for the purpose of listening to petitions for assistance and then provide support for our evolution. The sacred invocations within this book contain a basic energy formula that transforms stressful situations, transforms the people involved, and transforms us. This energy is infused with the qualities of the highest good and the highest wisdom. This holds true for anything we ask for within a sacred invocation, whether the invocation is for a past, present, or future event.

In the Creator's garden are the seeds of pure light. These pure lights are the angels and spirit guides themselves who have the sole purpose of crossing the span of time and space to help us. The atmosphere of sacred invocations creates an energetic petition to higher powers within the universe for intervention. These sacred invocations are always heard by our spirit helpers and angels who apply their wisdom and energy to resolve any given situation. I always learn much from these angels and spirit helpers who apply resolution energy to help in profound and wisdom-filled ways. I am amazed at the depth of wisdom these angels and spirit guides possess.

Angels are very different from humans. Even though they are different from us, they are in our lives to provide mentorship, healing, and intervention so we can evolve and become happy, mindful, able to enjoy our life here on Mother Earth. Angels can access many different dimensions and realms; we can also do this to a certain degree when we evolve. The angels and archangels work with qualities and evolved forms of energy. There are different types of angels and they have different roles and responsibilities. This information will be important when you need to invoke specialized angels and helpers throughout your life. All the kingdoms respond to angels when they are around. Even animals know the angels who possess the qualities of compassion, wisdom, and other virtues. You can feel their energy from a great distance away. The particles of energy around angels look like miniature soft orbs from a faraway galaxy and possess a golden colored energy, which is the highest form of energy and the highest form of thought. When angels speak, you receive not only the words but also all the wisdom from those words. Angels' words change the way you think of yourself and the way you see the world. You might have seen pictures of angels that have halos resting at the back of their heads; this is not a halo but rather a very pronounced moon chakra or moon energy center resting on the back of their head. It is made of the same energy you see when you view and experience a rainbow up close.

Angels are ethereal beings who possess the power of presenting themselves in various presentations depending on their purpose. They can appear in human forms when they are going to connect with humans directly. However, even in their natural state, they look similar to us in that they have a face and shoulders, and their moon center, which looks like a golden halo resting on the back of their head, is extremely pronounced.

I share the following story to better acquaint you on how angels work with us. When I was a young girl, I was sitting in a native teaching circle learning about the spirits of certain plants. It was a beautiful summer day and the warm sunset was blessing us with rays of orange amber light, and the campfire added calming silhouettes of fire and smoke. We started to sing native songs to awaken the medicine spirit of the plants, and I began to see small sparkles and spheres of light surrounding the plants we had in our hands. I felt the vibration of the plants as we placed the leaves into wooden bowls. Then, as I was sitting there, almost in a trance, I looked up and saw my teacher attentively listening to a beautiful image of a woman. This woman appeared like a white mist and in the color of a peaceful smoky white. She wore what appeared to be a cotton-like white robe, which gently flowed. It appeared as though she was making gentle recommendations to my teacher. I thought this beautiful vision was a play on my eyes because of the campfire, but I soon realized this was an angel, a special angel. She appeared friendly and her posture was like someone who was very knowledgeable. This angel had energy that felt like an old noble friend. She also observed our native teaching circle, and I could feel her heart fill with compassion for us. She wasn't from the world of humans; at least that was how I interpreted her. My feeling at that time was that she was there to provide comfort and advice. She was there for a period of time. Then she disappeared. I did not ask my teacher about her because I wasn't sure what he would say, and I wanted to process the experience by myself. Later, I learned she was an angel of the earth. These types of angels work with plants, crystals, and other elements on our planet.

As time went on, I encountered other angels and learned much about them. There are angels of the plant kingdom, there are earth angels that help with specific earthly things. There are angels of the sun, angels of the flowers, angels of the trees, angels of the crystal kingdom, angels of the water kingdom, and so much more.

Ever since I was a young girl, my visions of where they came from have been forever placed within my mind. Columns of light are the angels' homes, or at least a place where the angels sometimes reside. I am not sure why they use columns of light, but I feel it has something to do with traveling. The particles of energy that surround the angels are filled with nectars of wisdom, which are far beyond anything we could wrap our minds around. There is a lack of words to describe all of this, but the auras of angels are made of higher forms of wisdom. Human auras are mostly filled with past lives, traumas, beliefs, perceptions, and aspirations. Through human evolution and what is learned from these angels, auras will also evolve and possess pure wisdom.

When I was very young, I remember seeing an angel helping a traumatic situation. It was something I would never forget and it still impacts me to this day. Our family lived on a busy street. I was with my aunt when a car drove by very fast. I heard tires screech, and I realized something bad just happened. A car had run over and killed a small child who had run into the street. The old soul within me woke up. Suddenly, angelic information was coming into my mind and preparing me for what I was about to see.

I began to see a powerful column of light with particles of orbs near the child. The column of light turned into mist, like the clouds in the sky, and what came from this portal of light and mist was a very evolved being. It looked similar to a human but was made of particles of golden energy and white light. I knew this being was a special angel. I felt this angel's power and wisdom in every cell of my being. It was as if my entire energy field was standing at attention with honor and respect regarding the power and wisdom this angel carried. I knew the angel was there because of the child being hit by the car. There were three angels that manifested around the child and his mother. They were sending healing energy; it was coming out of the palms of their hands and the child's spirit was floating close to the lifeless body. I knew they were there to help, but I did not want to get too close because I was just a child myself, trying to understand what just happened.

The angels appeared to have a great sense of purpose. They were going to accompany the child's spirit. I was hiding behind my aunt because I did not want the angels to see me. If you can imagine being in the presence of powerful angels that have no limitations, it is a feeling that you can never forget. My mother came quickly and swooped me up, all three of us heading into the house. She guided all of us in a short prayer and then tried to keep us peaceful so we could release our emotions. This event still weighs on my mind to this very day.

Angels and spirit guides help humans for lots of reasons. One important reason is that all divine helpers, especially the archangels, have seen the great power and wisdom of the Great Spirit. These divine helpers are very committed to the Great Spirit's principles and divine plan. One of the principles of the Great Spirit is that all of creation be brought to its highest vibrational state. This can be done by the assistance and intervention of angels, divine helpers, virtuous teachers in spirit, and even family members on the other side. In the realm of angels and spirit guides, the heavenly realms vibrate at a very evolved frequency, which allows divine helpers to cross the spans of time, space, and realms. These helpers are able to travel due to a focused intention to provide the healing power of virtuous wisdom, thus transforming all events past, present, and future into their highest vibrational state. This means that when we ask for their help, they are very well equipped in knowledge, wisdom, and energetic tools to help a situation.

Inner plane helpers cross the veil to help humans gain maturity and enlightenment. They help us so we can bring traumas or stressful situations to a resolution, thus bringing healing, new knowledge, wholeness, and forgiveness occur. All events that occur in our lives do so in order to assist us in our evolution. What we learn from an event is just as valuable as the event itself. Where there is stress, there is focus; where there is focus, there is potential for resolution. With resolution, we free ourselves of ignorance in this lifetime and all other future lifetimes.

Our divine helpers have the gift of seeing all aspects of our situation and have the wisdom to provide great assistance to resolve our stress. Divine helpers can also transform energy into higher quality energy physically, emotionally, and mentally. I have experienced this so many times and have viewed many miracles for myself and others. When I was younger, a friend and her family moved into a house and soon found they were being harassed by ghosts. One day when I went to her house, I viewed it for myself. After seeing this ghoulish harassment, I wrote an invocation to ask my divine helpers to help my friend. She and I read the invocation together and then waited to see if anything would change.

A few days later, I received a strong feeling to come to her house. I knocked on her door and she answered. I asked her how she was doing and if anything changed in the house. She said it felt like something had. I told her we should sit in the house and read the invocation together again. We proceeded to do so and something powerful happened. We were in the living room, and we saw, in the middle of the house, a great light that grew brighter and brighter.

We experienced a feeling of the house being cleansed of energy. In my mind, I saw all the ghosts in the house guided to the beautiful, expanding light in the middle of the house. The ghosts were coming from so many places within the house into the light. Then, I saw beams of light coming from the expanding light. These beams turned into angels made of light. These angels went to places in the house and closed energetic doors (portals) where these ghosts were coming from. As the angels proceeded, I could feel the energy of the house becoming lighter, and the house was feeling so wonderful.

The beautiful expanding light in the middle of the house started to turn into sprinkles of small spheres of light and then disappeared. This all happened in a matter of what seemed moments, but I was so touched and moved by the experience. The angels gave me great comfort; their energy was incredibly beautiful and filled with divine substance. Both my friend and I were on the verge of tears because of the heavenly presence of these angels. Being in their presence awakened something inside of us that made us realize there is a powerful Creator. The Great Spirit's angels and divine helpers have an incredible presence.

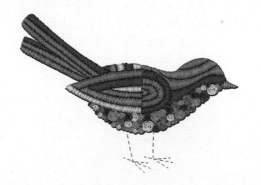

Chapter 3

THE SACRED POWER
OF INTENTION

Everyone has thoughts and utilizes some aspect of expressed desire, such as hope, and a general need or quality of wanting, which can be classified as an intention. Therefore, all of us have the capability of sending wonderful thoughts and intentions into the world, and to ourselves as well. Words make worlds, meaning that one of our important roles in this lifetime is to become aware of the qualities of energy we are bringing into our lives and into our world, thus creating the world we live in. Even though this book uses the power of words composed into an invocation, you can also replace the invocation techniques with wonderful sacred intentions and give permission to your virtuous energy and spirit guides to bring healing energy into this world.

As a young girl, I observed my mother, my father, and my elders demonstrate the power of intention. They also mentored me on the purpose of these practices. We would begin our mornings with a sacred intention. As a little girl, I would watch my mother and father as they closed their eyes and placed their hands on their heart centers. It was as if they were becoming one with a powerful source much higher than themselves. I was amazed to watch the energy around them change into something peaceful. This peaceful energy belonged to the Place of Light. It was as if my parents had picked up a hotline to speak to very powerful spirits in the energy world for the purpose of asking for their help, their guidance, and their intervention.

The sunrise and sunset were, and still are, special moments for our family. These times of day are when the Creator opens windows of time for us to receive energy from the spirit world and reconnect with the idea that we are pure energy. The stories at our sunrise and sunset ceremonies speak about the subtle energies of the spirit world, which can be accessed in so many ways. One way to access the spirit world is by closing our eyes. My native legends speak about this natural and simple gesture as a powerful posture that connects us with our medicine spirit. When we close our eyes, we are accessing the world of energy. Closing our eyes allows us to focus our attention inward into our spirit.

The power of a morning sunrise ceremony includes the power of intention, which will adjust our energy field through our sacred intentions. I was taught that our energy field will adjust itself in order to navigate and provide guidance to help us achieve our expressed desires through our sacred intentions. When I was younger, we practiced this by starting our mornings with mindful intentions that were carefully directed by our elders. Our energy field can navigate itself through the power of our intentions and the power of our thoughts, especially if those intentions have elevated perspectives, sentiments, feelings, and beliefs.

A sacred intention is a gift from the Great Spirit, a beautiful energy tool that accesses all energy realms. The landscape of the mind has many avenues regarding qualities of thoughts, emotions, and contemplations. A focused thought from the center of our heart and spirit that has a higher vibration of intention is most certainly a sacred intention and a very important part of this book. We often have thoughts about our day, but when we think about someone or something we love and express a wonderful quality of energy toward them, we are creating a sacred intention. This sacred intention starts in the energy world first and then takes its journey of manifestation into our physical world. Energy that is created from our beautiful light and spirit carries the energy of healing and can be used anywhere and any realm because energy crosses the span of time and space. Infinite wisdom, which is another way we address the Creator, is most wise to create time and energy, as they are conduits for us in many ways. A thought is an energy carrier, and the energy of thought is part of the formula to manifest and bring qualities into this world. The goal of the universe is to help guide us to bring energy into this world wisely and mindfully. My teacher said that while we are here on the earth, we are learning how to move energy through us. By choosing and learning the various qualities of energy, we can mindfully bring energy into our lives and the world and make it a lifelong journey.

A peaceful mind, sacred and peaceful breath, and our expressed desire of having something heal or reach a better vibration are all components of a sacred intention. One of the most important parts is to have a belief that our sacred intention will not only be heard but that it will be answered. Sometimes it is through mentoring us and awakening us so we can approach our intention with knowledge and activities in line with these sacred intentions. You are made of virtuous light, which is the essence of who you are. Your energy can change the vibration of the earth and regions of land, neighborhoods, and living spaces. This book has the benefit of helping you become more conscious of your creations and also realize the various energies you can bring into this world. When we become awakened and aware that Mother Earth is a learning place, as well as a beautiful world to enjoy, the potential of healing and wellness for your life is endless. As you review this book you will begin to mindfully navigate energy for yourself and others—meaning our families, other people, plants, animals, Mother Earth, past, present, and even our future. As we become more thoughtful about how we navigate energy, we reconnect with our virtuous power to create. Universal life force flows through us to help others dynamically. My teacher said that we will always create, whether we have a physical body or just a spirit in the energy world. The key is to create mindfully and wisely.

With all of that in mind, here is a step-by-step procedure to generate a sacred intention: Sanction at least fifteen minutes of uninterrupted time where you will not be distracted. Find a comfortable position and keep a pen and paper with you in case you want to record your insights. Focus on your breath and connect with a part of nature near you, maybe the ebb and flow of the water or the wind blowing by. This is so your breath becomes one with the timing of that aspect of nature. Once your breath syncs into the rhythm of that aspect of nature, continue to allow the breath to be filled with peace. Send blessings to the water, the birds, the trees, the air, and the animals.

Use the less predominant hand and place it on your heart. Focus your mind on your heart and the top of the head. Contemplate a virtuous desire such as sending virtuous energy to your neighborhood or home for the purpose of peace and harmony. Visualize white light permeating from you and from the sky to your neighborhood or home with the quality you have chosen, such as peace and harmony. See everyone and everything accepting this wonderful energy; visualize people taking a moment and placing their hands on their heart and becoming brighter and brighter within their energy field.

Add to your intention that you wish for the wonderful energy of peace and harmony to continue to permeate your neighborhood or home more and more and on a daily basis. An added benefit is to ask wonderful angels to continue to transform the neighborhood or home into peace, harmony, and virtuous wisdom.

Take a deep breath and express gratitude for the blessings that are on their way. Very gently open your eyes. You've just completed not only creating a sacred intention but, also, you've sent that wonderful intention to your neighborhood or home.

Thoughts carry energy and the goal of this book is to help develop the understanding and knowledge that our energetic purpose is to navigate energy with higher qualities of wisdom. When we do this, something very special happens. A blossoming of evolution and healing occurs for all of us. Every single person is a teacher, you are teaching yourself and teaching others by your pure presence. Energy crosses the span of time. The universe wants us to evolve so we can assist and participate in creating wonderful energy on Mother Earth.

I define energy as a mechanism by which it continues to manifest a platform of possibilities. Thus, we manifest through the thoughts, feelings, images, and intentions we maintain within our energy field consistently. This is done through intensity of thought and duration of thought, which manifests an outcome. With this knowledge we start to realize that we can have happiness, peace, and great productivity in our lives and in our surroundings.

This book will help you connect with your spirit helpers who are wisdom filled and can help bring out the best of all situations within our lives. Enjoy this book, as it contains many personal mystical stories to help you connect with the power of their wonderful assistance.

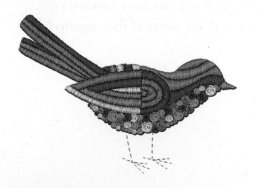

Chapter 4

THE START OVER CEREMONY

In the Apache tradition, there's a ceremony that is done during various times of the moon cycles called the Start Over Ceremony. I am sharing this information with you so you can use these techniques in your daily routine to promote a greater sense of being centered and to invoke your wisdom.

Before beginning any ceremony, it's important to start with a special practice called *the seven invisible breaths*. The seven invisible breaths can be applied in our daily life. I would recommend that you apply this practice every morning to recalibrate your internal energy compass. I believe you will find the seven invisible breaths very useful. I welcome you to use the practice prior to making a decision, attending an important meeting, searching for an answer, or finding inspiration. It could even be used prior to a meditation and even before sleeping.

My native tradition has taught us that when we close our eyes, we are going into the spirit world of more subtle energy. Therefore, please close your eyes during this following practice of the seven breaths. The first step is to gently close the eyes and focus on the breath. Do not change the breath, just observe it and see it in your mind's eye. Send a blessing to the trees, the clouds, the water, and the animals. The second step is to think of a teacher who has touched your life for the better. Send a blessing to that teacher and say thank you. For the third step, clear the energy of your aura and the energy in the area surrounding you. This is done by taking a deep breath, and as you exhale, feel the power of wind spirits sweeping your aura and the immediate area with brilliant white light. The fourth step is to call forth your wisdom self, speak out loud, and say, "I call forth my wisdom self, to be front and center. Guide me today. Thank you." In the fifth step, call forth your energetic resources, which are your personal guides, helpers, virtuous ancestors, and teachers in spirit, to be with you today. They will help you and you will learn so much from their assistance. Have patience with these beings and you will establish more clarity within your life.

For step six, visualize your medicine place. Create a place in your mind where you feel supported, loved, and divinely guided. I always visualize myself with my mother, sitting in the middle of a very ancient medicine wheel on top of sacred mountains. I can feel and see my guides, teachers, spirit helpers, plant medicine spirits, and even the sun surrounding us with beautiful energy. I feel loved, supported, protected, and surrounded by wisdom. In the seventh step, invoke your sacred intention for the day. Then, observe your breath again and take note that your breath has changed in a good way. Try to keep this breath throughout the day. This is the breath of ceremony. Use this practice to rebalance yourself throughout the day to help you facilitate wisdom.

The Start Over Ceremony I am about to share with you is something you can use to connect with your wisdom-self and your virtuous helpers, and to provide insight for something that is happening in your life.

The Start Over Ceremony is done in a circle, which represents the symbolic presentation of giving and receiving. I believe that giving back to the earth by expressing deep gratitude and great care of Mother Earth is so very important, so the circle represents harmony, peace, gratitude, and the Great Spirit. The four directions of east, west, north, and south are honored by positioning elders who hold those directions within the Start Over Ceremony. The next step is to sing several ceremonial songs with drums, after which we go into a quiet state and speak to the Creator and to our divine helpers.

During this quiet moment we say, "Dear Great Spirit, this is what transpired in my life that needs more insight, more healing, and your blessing." State what happened, how you responded, then ask for more insight. Also, list the things you learned, the speak about all the things you would do differently with the qualities of evolution and enlightenment given to you by the Creator. The final step is to ask the Creator if there is anything else you need to understand or do differently.

Once these steps take place, a window of energy will move into the ceremony space to bring the wisdom and the insight about resolving the questions asked in the previous paragraph. Then, express gratitude for the virtuous wisdom received.

The reason why I shared this ceremony with you is because the universe would like very much for all of us to become awakened and enlightened, so that all events—past, present, and future—can bring their highest vibrational states of wisdom and evolution. When we become wise, we become happy and utilize our beautiful capabilities for ourselves and others in good and virtuous ways. Thus, we become prosperous, honoring, joyful, healthy, and all the things that we would love to have in our lives are there to enjoy.

Here is how you can apply the Start Over Ceremony on your own. Sanction at least twenty minutes of uninterrupted time. Sit quietly and focus on your breath. See yourself sitting within a medicine wheel or circle, and connect with the clouds, sky, earth, mountains, birds, trees, and water. Send all these parts of nature a blessing. Invoke for the shaman within you to be present and to provide you with wisdom and helpful insights. Share with your inner shaman your current situation and speak the following: "Here is the current situation and here is what I did. Here is what I learned; here is what I would do differently. Is there anything else I need to learn and do about this situation?" Release these spoken words and quietly focus on the breath. Gently allow for the answer to come. If it does not come right away, be patient because the information comes to you when you least expect it. When this happens, remember to express gratitude and thank your guides and the shaman within you.

This is Sacred Balance, and it is my goal in this book to help you to learn how to use energy in a thoughtful, wisdom-filled, and virtuous way.

While we are here on Mother Earth, we are learning to move energy through us and add wonderful qualities of energy into our journey and the journey of others. We are navigators of energy.

Chapter 5

GRANDFATHER'S WISDOM WORDS

This chapter welcomes you to receive insight and training from a native elder regarding the power of medicine words and why they exist and are used within the invocations in this book. This chapter also explains how to use this information to resolve stressful or confusing situations in our lives.

Grandfather said that some words carry Light, the Light of the Creator. These medicine words carrying this Light open channels that act like conduits to facilitate the light of the Creator. These words allow the Great Spirit's medicine helpers to cross the span of time and space to help and transform situations, events, and people. It is a way of harnessing the wonderful substance of energy for the good of things here on Mother Earth. Grandfather also shared that some words carry darkness and lower vibration energy, which promote disorientation, fear, illness, depression, addictions, turbulence, and even violence. Words that carry Light are healing, and promote wisdom, virtuous insights, mental enlightenment, Sacred Balance, peace, inspiration, and empowered energy that removes darkness, removes lower vibrational energy, and connects us to the powerful source of the Creator.

Grandfather shared with me many wonderful native traditions, ceremonies, and wisdom. One thing that stands out to me, and launched me to build my wellness practice, was studying the energy of evolved words called *enlightened language*. This language maps out energy and allows the realm of energy helpers to cross the span of time and space to help us.

I have learned to experience and utilize this wonderful energy, and this has taught me fresh wisdom each day. Grandfather said the Great Spirit gifted us with the power of words and the guiding principle of words to create access points to the realm of the Creator's divine helpers: the place of healing and the place of wisdom. The Great Spirit designed the platform of energy as a conduit for manifesting all aspects of things. Grandfather said if we use words like medicine, they become medicine for all things past, present, and future for ourselves, and also provide assistance for others: people, plants, or animals.

During the ceremonies, grandfather and other elders would use enlightened language to speak with their spirit guides, teachers in spirit, ancestors, angels, Grandmother Moon, the spirit of plants, the animal kingdom, and even the Creator. Enlightened language is the positioning of words that have an abundance of Light. The qualities and vibrations of these words allow for the opening of energy portals to establish a connection to the Place of Light, a place where our spirit helpers reside. This is one of the reasons why we sing sacred songs with drums, which were taught to us so we could adjust the energy around us during ceremonies.

The concept of enlightened language always intrigued me, as I often watched my grandfather use this language, filled with Light, to position himself in such a way as to energetically retrieve wisdom, insight, healing energy, and so much more. His wisdom was profound, powerful, and transforming.

I once asked my grandfather how I could acquire wisdom, insight, and knowledge for my life's journey by learning and using enlightened language. He said, first and foremost, in order to develop a quality that will allow evolution, it is important to express a desire for it. He instructed me to write an energetic narrative to invoke enlightened qualities to come into my energy field. He said I needed to make this request with my heart and soul. When I did this, I received a downpour of information and insight.

Grandfather told me that the Great Spirit gifted us the power of medicine words that contain Light to access our helpers in the spirit world. These words were also gifted to us in order to help us achieve the principle of Sacred Balance in everything we do. The Great Spirit infused Mother Earth with the gift of sacred timing. When we are in nature, we are touched and influenced by this sacred timing, which promotes healing and syncs our internal timing to promote balance. This helps all of us become connected to words that have Light.

Grandfather added this wonderful piece of wisdom: The world of our ancestors, the world of our spirit guides, and the world of our divine helpers dwell in the vibration and quality of their world of wisdom. Thus, the words that contain Light that we use to invoke these helpers connect us with them. These words bring wonderful energy and powerful helpers into our world to provide their help. The medicine words that contain Light are within the energetic narratives called *invocations*.

My grandfather had many examples of this powerful principle. One of them was the story of a man named John, who at the age of thirteen began a four-year journey of being traumatized by a bully in high school. This caused John to experience depression for many years, even into college. Grandfather instructed John to read a sacred invocation for resolution every night. Approximately eight weeks after meeting with my grandfather, John was surprised to see, standing directly in front of him, the bully from so many years ago. The bully said to John, "I wonder if you remember me. I use to go to high school with you. I would like to apologize for the wrong I did to you, and I apologize with all my heart for what I did."

John felt, both physically and emotionally, something very profound. He felt much energy being lifted from different areas in his body. When the bully apologized, he lifted the affliction of his harsh actions toward John.

What John experienced was the power of healing medicine words, which facilitated for John's aura the powerful energetic release of trauma from his energy field. What quickly followed, in that moment, was an experience of great lightness in his body, mind, and spirit. He also experienced an epiphany about the situation and had a moment of understanding that we are all a part of something greater than ourselves.

At another level, these invocations specifically call forth the assistance of very enlightened beings to enlist their wisdom-filled work with the event to bring all energies, persons, and situations to their highest vibrational state. Invocations are not only used to resolve things that have happened in our past and present, but also create new things to come into our life. I will speak more about this in the next chapter, where a medicine woman uses invocations to see into the future.

Chapter 6

MEDICINE WOMAN'S WISDOM WORDS

This chapter will provide you with information on how the medicine woman uses the power of words within special invocations to access future information and brings fresh knowledge and new wisdom from the future into this moment in time. This will help you to utilize more advanced invocations that will help you during stressful situations. This different approach to invocations can add great value to your efforts of achieving levels of expertise, awareness, fresh insights, and specific qualities needed within our careers, relationships, and wellness. I will share some examples and supportive personal stories to help you utilize this advanced method of using invocations.

The examples within this chapter—regarding the medicine woman and how she provided the extra value of seeing into the future to further assist her tribal members—can be used as good counsel for our life's journey. These examples show that invocations can help us develop skills, talents, and qualities within this lifetime.

The medicine woman often used specific advanced invocations to access the spirit world to learn new skills needed for the survival of tribal members. When you use a medicine woman invocation to bring new future skills into this lifetime, you may experience extraordinary insights throughout the day. I recommend keeping a journal to secure a good place for your notes and insights you receive. Keeping notes in your journal will help you fine-tune new skills you are looking to develop.

Another interesting feature of using this advanced form of invocations is unique dream time information which is provided by your personal guides to help support the skill you are looking to attain. I suggest that you keep dream notes within your journal about these dreams to help support your medicine woman invocation. Also, if you receive information through your dreams that requires more understanding, please take time to ask questions about the information during your meditations. Meditation provides our mind a wonderful place to ask questions regarding all the new information you are receiving.

One of the important items the medicine woman brings to the tribe and to the world is an interesting new fresh application about energetic narratives that come from her spirit guides and teachers in spirit. The qualities of the feminine wisdom energy that are shared within this book are the wonderful profound insight about how energetic narratives can be used to assist and empower our future by developing fresh new skills, new knowledge, and new proficiencies for this lifetime and the next. This is the direction the medicine woman guides us toward to contemplate and utilize, to imagine what you want which is new and fresh in our lives. You can most certainly ask for this from your spirit guides through energetic narratives. You can also ask to be mentored during sleep time to learn virtuous things from divine helpers to help step into careers that might take lifetimes to learn.

I remember my teachers telling me that there is a significant amount of people who never have new thoughts about themselves. They have the same thoughts each day and these repeated thoughts have created their past and will most certainly create their future. My teacher said if we want a new direction in our lives, it is important to have new thoughts to pave the way to new callings in our life. That being said, the medicine woman developed the idea and concept to use energetic narratives to help approach and design a wonderful, fresh way to gain new knowledge and new awareness by being virtuously mentored during our sleep time with our wonderful guides and divine helpers. You will find within this book useful and profound energetic narratives called sacred invocations to connect with your divine helpers and receive fresh ideas, fresh wisdom, healing energies, and courage to step into your wonderful purpose. In other words, you can use the invocations within this book and also develop skills to write your own invocations. I share some wonderful examples of these energetic narratives within this book.

The medicine woman examples utilize the power of healing words to focus and solidify resolution to the past, present, and the future. I remember my teacher sharing with me that time is a gift from the Creator. Time is used for many things; however, my teacher shared that when we think of something that happened to us many years ago, it is no longer in the past, but rather, that event, that memory, is in the here and now and is present within our mind now. And because it is in the here and now, it can be reshaped and provided with many qualities of energy. We can reshape and provide qualities of energy to every past moment. The Great Spirit provided the power of transformation of all past events through the time element, an invocation for the principle of evolution. It is said, the Creator requests all past events to be brought to the highest potential of energy so we can evolve and awaken ourselves and others.

Resolving our past and even present stressful situations in our life's journey is so very important, taking into consideration that each time we do so we are affecting the book of life for our current journey and affecting our future lifetimes. With every thought, feeling, image, and words that we express, we are actually adjusting our future and our past in such a wonderful way. Finding meaning and purpose in our lives protects us from despair, fear, anger, hatred, and all the lower vibrations. The medicine woman teaches that reconnecting with the traditional ways heals our spirit, our soul, our journey.

Grandmother said that words are an expression of self-care. The Creator blessed us with medicine in the form of words that carry Light, which would most certainly heal us at many levels, but even at the basic level this medicine trickles down. Even when we write in our journals or write a story of what happened to us, something magical happens, such as, helping us express ourselves, organize our thoughts, emotions, concerns, and even track our progress. Words have the potential even at the basic level of journaling to facilitate mindfulness and self-awareness. We begin to understand that words are carriers of energy.

Having said this, the extra value the medicine woman brings to this concept is the principle of using energetic narratives called invocations to develop skills, talents, and qualities that we would like to have. Our elders would use certain words to connect with our divine helpers and the Great Spirit. This is called elevated language and sometimes called elevated enlightened words, which are used in an invocation to bring to us virtuous mentors to help us develop virtuous skills to integrate into our life's purpose and careers. Thus, the advanced form of energetic narratives was created.

I'd like to share a very insightful personal story about the concept of using sacred invocations to receive future energy, future information, and future training. Many years ago, my younger sister wasn't feeling very well and secured an appointment with her internal medicine doctor. He ran the typical tests, found she had cancer, and gave a diagnosis of stage four pancreatic cancer and liver cancer. Both her internal medicine doctor and oncologist stated that she was too far along and did not recommend chemotherapy and radiation. They felt she was not strong enough for these protocols and treatments. The doctors, also feeling she was too far along for treatment to be effective, only gave her three months to live. She reached out to me, and we talked over the phone. I felt her sadness and urgency to receive some type of a miracle. My heart was filled with love and concern for her. Yes, I did very much want to help her. I did indeed provide her with energy work and a healthy diet and other herbs which would help her get stronger. However, I knew there was more information in the energy world which might help her. So, I wrote an energetic narrative and asked for assistance from the spirit world to help my sister.

I read my invocation every night, and on the third night when I awoke from my sleep in the morning, I felt a deep need to read my invocation again and then do a meditation to possibly receive a message from the spirit world. I asked before I began my meditation for new insight, wisdom, training and mentoring to help my sister. Something very powerful happened: I proceeded to do a meditation and during my meditation I heard a virtuous voice from the spirit world that said, *Isn't it interesting that people always say they wish they knew then what they know now, and things might have been different.*

Then something interesting happened. My mind immediately went into a great stillness because this profound statement took me into a time and space that allowed me to understand I was being given a powerful piece of information which would help me decipher what they were trying to share with me. I quietly spoke the words out loud and focused my breath into a place of peace. As I

repeated the words of this statement over and over—I suddenly
received a huge and powerful insight regarding what I heard in the
spirit world. *Yes! I understand now.*

My mind thought about the principle of time. Grandfather said
time was a gift from the Great Spirit which can be used in many
ways regarding the past, present, and future. I also thought about
how the medicine woman received the great insight to use her training to write energetic narratives to develop skills and qualities that
are within our future lifetimes, and that we can ask to be mentored
to secure these qualities in the here and now. All this and so much
more was pouring into my mind. I then took a deep breath and said
"By the power of my good merits, I invoke to receive wonderful wisdom and techniques that I will know ten years in the future that
might have helped my sister. Bring this information and wisdom to
me right now. And by the power of my good merits, whatever I will
learn ten years from now in the future about how to help my sister—bring it to me now at all levels bring that information, wisdom,
and techniques to me, here and now."

Suddenly, it was as if my spirit and consciousness energetically
travelled ten years into my future and extracted that information, re-
trieving this information from the future and bringing it to me as I
was sitting there in my meditation chair. Suddenly, I felt my mind
open to endless amounts of information which started pouring
into my head and I immediately started writing as fast as I could.
I learned so very much and everything made wonderful sense. I
could feel this wisdom enter every cell of my brain and consciousness. From this information I began to develop and utilize a specialized form of energy work which I designed and utilized for my sister—plus, some traditional applications of Apache water infusions
which I am writing about to make it available to the public in my
next book. The new design of energy work, with specific medita-

tion practices and nutrition, truly helped my sister and together we worked to compile it for others. I also taught this specialized form of energy work at the Cancer Treatment Center in Zion, Illinois, to their mind-body division and their pain division. I called it Oncology Reiki; it was very useful, and I am currently writing a book that combines all the information I received to help my sister, which was a combination of Native American plant medicine nutrition, healing energy work; and meditation practices, as well as using energetic narratives to help guide the energy. My sister did indeed get healthier, so much so that her doctors agreed to allow for the chemo protocol, which was her desire and wish. Even during the first stages of the chemotherapy she demonstrated via the blood work that no tumor markers were found. Please note that energetic narratives do not replace medical care and medical intervention.

This personal story is a great example on how medicine woman invocations can work. Enjoy the following chapters, which contain various invocations that can be used to not only resolve things in the past and present, but also future skills to bring into our life in the here and now.

Part Two

INVOCATIONS

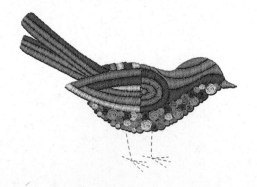

CLEAN AN ENERGY FIELD

What is an energy field? An energy field is often called an *aura*. According to my native teachings, the energy field is a gift from the Great Spirit that contains special navigation tools within it, as well as energy particles selected by you in your past lives. Energy fields can also carry aspirations for future endeavors. Generally, our energy fields are guided by our thoughts, words, feelings, proclivities, and actions, all of which direct our life journeys. However, an energy field can be affected by the thoughts and actions of others. We all get a little dusty from the trail, so to speak. Cleansing an energy field will help to see the world with clarity and provide vitality to every aspect of ourselves. When energy gets congested, the flow of energy—also called the *river of life*—gets stagnant and begins to lack vitality. Vitality is a valuable factor, which is why it is essential to clear an energy field of particles and forces that may infringe upon our well-being at all levels.

Energy fields have many functions and qualities. The first primary function of the energy field is to provide us with information for our survival. A good example of this is taking a nature walk within your neighborhood and suddenly getting the sense that someone is watching you. As you turn to look around, you do indeed find someone staring at you. How did this information come to you? Your aura provided this information to you. Your energy field has within it a basic operating system that conveys information to you about your whereabouts to help keep you safe.

A secondary function of an energy field is to bring vitality into all aspects of who you are: physical, emotional, spiritual, and mental. An energy field does this by extracting the energy from the sun, the air, the earth, the water, crystals, food, medicine, thoughts about yourself, and even blessings sent to you by other people.

A third function of an energy field is to provide healing to the past lives you select to work on during this lifetime by providing events and situations within your daily life to give you the potential to evolve.

A fourth function of the energy field is to be of service and help you accomplish your life's purpose. An example of this fourth function is to think about a time when you helped someone and how great you felt when they thanked you. This fills our energy field with universal life force because we provided a healing service to someone in a wisdom-filled way.

The fifth important function of the energy field is that it contains energy of future aspirations one may have selected to develop within this lifetime.

A sixth, more advanced, function of the energy field is that it is an energy navigation tool to direct positive healing energy to ourselves and other sentient beings. It is important to learn how to navigate our energy fields because our fields can facilitate a significant amount of beneficial universal life force energy. A good example of this principle is using a sacred intention in the morning that adjusts our energy field through our words. This modifies an energy field to seek out what we need to help us during the day. Some people may know this practice as a Native American sunrise ceremony, where thanks is given to the Creator and the natural world. This practice also includes a request for certain things to occur during the day and to be guided with the powerful energy of the Creator and the Creator's divine helpers. This practice adjusts energy fields in order to obtain the requests we've given to energy fields and spirit guides.

A seventh function of the energy field is the quality of realization that we may be viewing the world around us with tinted glasses, so to speak. This seventh function is for receiving powerful energy from the source of the Place of Light. My native teachings tell me that we have access and are entitled to the divine life source we came from. We do this by honoring and respecting nature, because nature is not only the doorway to our wellness but also the doorway to our spirituality. Why is this? Nature has never lost its connection with the Great Spirit and spirit guides. The trees, plants, mountains, water, sky all breathe in Sacred Balance and help us to connect to our own Sacred Balance and spirit. The trees, plants, mountains, water, sky all breathe; we all breathe together. This native concept helps us to walk through life with a more evolved energy.

Everyone is healing from something, and when we experience congested energy or non-beneficial energy in our energy fields, we may react in a constrictive and emotionally harmful way.

The eighth, and final, function of the energy field is to learn to become a conduit of various evolved qualities and energies. This function is meant to keep our energy field clean and clear of harmful energy. As we work with our energy fields, we may also start to realize we can do this for others. When our energy field is clearer and filled with positive energy, we experience vitality. We think clearly and move in the world with more wisdom.

I recommend clearing your own energy field twice a day. I invite you to try it and feel the difference. The invocation that follows will ask for special angels and divine helpers to help us remove harmful energies, non-virtuous entities, and other congested qualities from our energy field, or aura. The invocation will also ask for our virtuous helpers and special angels, called the *medics*, to help. My teacher introduced me to these divine helpers. Their jobs are to take lower vibration energy or harmful energy off our energy field and take it to receive healing medicine in the energy world so all harmful energies can be transformed into virtuous energy.

My teacher Mama Little Wolf always said, "We all get a little dusty from the trail." Yes, no doubt we do get a little dusty from the trail. In other words, our energy gets impacted from all the energy that is around us. Mama Little Wolf would often talk about energy and how energy can travel through time and space. She was right; we are all swimming in energy and sometimes our energy field gets a little congested from interacting with traumas, daily stress, emotional people, and other overwhelming issues. We can also be energetically affected by the energy of our past life experiences, as well as the energy within our environments.

An example of using this invocation is on soldiers that return home from war. They have seen violence, harmful actions, injustices, and trauma. These types of negative energies have the potential to remain within their energy fields. For the soldiers, the feeling of these energies is very much like carrying heavy burdens and harmful motion pictures actively playing in their mind. This does not allow happiness and peace during daily and nightly activities. It is important to energetically remove these traumas that reside within the energy field. For traumas such as these, those who understand the use of invocations can facilitate an important ceremony that cleanses the soldiers' energy fields to remove the traumatic images and harsh energies. This helps them acclimate back into society and their families. This is an excellent example of why we need to clean our energy field to promote vitality and wisdom. Cleaning our energy field is similar to a nutrient or a vitamin to keep us healthy to support wisdom-filled thoughts.

The following invocation is a great technique to clean an energy field. I use it daily. I would also recommend a purification practice, as an option, to additionally clean your energy field. The purification practice within this chapter is purely optional, but also very helpful.

Please read the following invocation when you feel your energy field needs a nice energy cleansing and you need a positive energy boost. This invocation is also helpful when you are stressed, upset, having a bad day, or even when you feel fatigued. It is also helpful to use this invocation when multiple things feel as though they are going awry. It is always best to read it out loud. You can also place the text of this invocation in your wallet to have it handy when needed. It is always best to read it quietly and with as much focus as possible.

Invocation to Clean Our Energy Field

By the power of my good merits, I invoke for the medics to pick up all non-virtuous forces, all mental illness forces, all non-virtuous entities, all mental illness entities from people, noxious energies, and other planes of existence that have affected me, and have the medics take these non-virtuous forces to receive medical care in the entities' world, never to return to me or anyone else. Fill the void from which they were removed with divine light, divine love, and virtuous uplifting wisdom, safety, and virtuous vitality for me. Here and now and from this day forward, physically, mentally, emotionally, and at all other levels.

Also, if there is any past life debt, please secure its resolution gently and without harm to me or anyone involved and supply all with healing medicine in the energy world, using the quality of peace, wholeness, forgiveness, and divine energy. In full faith, here and now, and from this day forward, thank you.

Cleanse Your Energy Field with Smoke Purification Practice

To begin this sacred Smoke Purification Practice to help purify our energy field of negative energy, start by sanctioning approximately twenty to thirty minutes of uninterrupted time where you can totally focus on yourself.

Decide on a quiet place where you can sanction a peaceful time to implement this practice. You can do this in your home, a meditation area, or anywhere you feel comfortable and safe.

Begin by having a virtuous intention as to what you would like to achieve and list out some of the things that are currently stressful for you. Also, contemplate and list out events and situations you feel agitated, overwhelmed, or disturbed about. Create a very simple sacred intention in your mind that you are going to move all these blocks and obstacles and negative energies off your energy field and away from your journey of life. Replace it with wisdom and wellness for yourself and others.

Set up all your smoke purification tools, which may include an abalone shell or a heat-resistant bowl to burn your dried herbs. Herbs should include dried lavender, lemon balm, purple sage, cedar, or dried juniper. All these plants carry healing energies when burned.

Take a nice deep breath in through your nose, exhale through your mouth, again breathing in through your nose and exhaling through your mouth. As you breathe in, breathe in the breath of life. As you exhale, release all the tension in your body. Take your less dominant hand and place it on your heart. Place a smile on your face and one hand over your tools and make a prayer. Focus on your heart center and also the top of your head, which is your crown center. Maintain a relaxed smile on your face and say the following: "By the power of my good merits, I invoke my virtuous teachers in spirit and all the virtuous beings who assist me. Please send your virtuous energy through me to infuse my cleansing tools and myself with your virtuous healing energy. In full faith, so be it now."

Next, take a pinch of the dried herbs and raise it up to the sky and ask for the universe to infuse it with divine light. Take a pinch of the cedar raised it up to the sky, make a prayer, and ask the universe and your divine helpers to infuse the cedar with divine light. Say thank you and return the herb back into the bowl. Next, take a pinch of the dried lavender and raise it up to the sky and ask for the universe to infuse it with divine light. Next, ask for your divine helpers to infuse it with divine light. Hold it there for a moment, and then say thank you and place it back in the bowl. Continue in this same procedure with all the dried herbs. If you have other dried herbs, do the same procedure.

After you have completed this process, take a match and light the combination of dried plants within the abalone shell or your heat-resistant bowl. Use your hand to fan the smoke and make sure the fire goes out. The smoke will begin to encompass the bowl and the area around it. Make a prayer and ask for the smoke and the spirit of the plants to clean and purify your energy field. Use an open hand and fan and move the smoke from the top of your head all the way down to your feet. Use additional smoke to cover any areas you feel need extra cleansing. If the smoke goes out, take time to light the dried plants again to generate more smoke. If you need to add more cedar, lavender, lemon balm, and purple sage, you're welcome to do so at any time.

Proceed to cleanse your chakras. Start at the top of your head, which is the crown chakra, and move down. You will proceed to the third eye in the area of the forehead, then the throat chakra, which is in the area of the throat, then the heart chakra, which is in the area of the heart center. Keep moving down, cleansing the solar plexus, which is in the area of the stomach, followed by the pelvis and also, if possible, to reach around and do the tailbone. If you cannot reach your tailbone and your back, you can use your mind and picture yourself in front of you and cleanse the back of your head, the back of your neck, your spine, your tailbone, your legs, and your feet. While you are cleansing yourself with the smoke, use your internal voice to mentally describe how you are cleansing every aspect of your energy field, every aspect of your mind, body, and spirit, and purifying yourself at all levels with this cleansing ceremony.

Here is a short affirmation you can use when you are cleansing yourself with the smoke: "Into this smoke, I cleanse myself of all negativity. I ask for this plant spirit smoke to remove all harmful energies and take them up to the spirit world for healing medicine. Fill my mind, body, and spirit with divine light, divine love, and divine peace. I cleanse myself fully, so that every aspect of myself is in Sacred Balance. I am in deep gratitude to the plant kingdom for helping me. Blessings to the plant kingdom and my divine helpers. Fill my energy field with cleansing smoke and take away all negativity and fill me with all the divine virtues of peace, goodness, and positive energy. In full faith, so be it now, thank you."

If you need to add more dried plants into your abalone shell, you are welcome to do this at any time.

After you have completed cleansing your entire body with the smoke, hold the bowl with one hand on each side and express gratitude to the universe, your virtuous helpers, the plant kingdom, your wisdom self, and all the wonderful beings who assist you in good and virtuous ways. You are welcome to use the following short closing prayer: "By the power of my good merits, I express deep gratitude to the universe, to my virtuous divine helpers, to the plant kingdom, to my wisdom self, and all the wonderful beings who assist me in good and virtuous ways. Please continue to purify and cleanse my energy field; bless me so I can be a blessing to others. In full faith, so be it now, thank you."

Place your hands on your heart center, close your eyes, take a nice deep breath in through your nose, exhale through your mouth. Use this breath pattern several times. Within your mind, say, *Thank you, I am super receptive and super conductive and accept this virtuous energy for my wellness so that I may move through this world with wisdom and wellness. So be it now.*

Take time to be connected to all your divine helpers and the plant kingdom, your higher self, and also see your energy field becoming very bright in your mind's eye. Very gently open your eyes and adjust yourself back into your surroundings by looking around using a peaceful smile on your face, and experience the energy and quality of gratitude for a moment.

You have completed the smoke purification practice to clean and purify your energy field. Take time to clean your smoke purification tools. If there are any dried herbs left in your smoke purification bowl or abalone shell, please take time to take them outside and return them to Mother Earth. Do so by placing all remaining dried herbs in a safe area, such as an area where rocks or sand is present. This is important, so any remaining dried herbs do not accidentally catch fire. Then, wipe your abalone shell and, or smoke purification bowl and return it back into a place that holds your tools until the next time you need them. I like to wrap my bowl and dried plants in an organic white cotton cloth and then place these special items in a unique or personal box, which contains my special energy tools. You can place your special energy tool box in your meditation area or wherever you keep your energy tools.

ENERGETIC BOUNDARIES AND PROTECTION

Most people have come to realize that the energy of others can affect us either in a positive way or a negative way. The importance of setting energetic boundaries means we can be around people, especially family, and set our intentions and advocate our needs without stressing ourselves out. We may not realize it, but energy is very real.

This chapter provides directions on how we can use an invocation to set energetic boundaries and protect our aura from depletion. An excellent example can be made with two people who have an intense argument in a room and, several hours later, when a different person comes into that very same room, that person feels a great sense of agitation and anger within the room. Let's take another example: maybe a war occurred many years ago in a region of land. Now, everyone who lives on that land feels the residual trauma in various forms of emotions and energy. Also, hospitals are notorious for having stressful and depleting energy because of all the traumas and emotions left there by patients and their families. This is not to mention doctors who are stressed and nurses who are overworked. Then, there are deeper aspects of energy from past lives and hardships that impact our lives.

My teacher shared a wonderful insight about energetic boundaries, which helps us see how energy works between people. In the example he used Point A and Point B.

Point A is one person and Point B is another person and in between Point A and Point B is a stream of energy. This stream of energy that exists between one person and another can be inappropriate energy or appropriate energy, which influences how we relate to each other. Think of your relationship with food. We can have an inappropriate relationship with food, or we can have the appropriate relationship with food which will help us maintain our ideal weight. Each person contributes to the quality of the energy that flows between them.

There is a very old story about some of the universal principles that are at play here. The universe and the Creator want all energies from our past, present, and even our future to be brought to the highest quality of energy. We have the power to change the quality of the energy that flows between us and our surroundings; thus, changing the quality of the relationship and this flow of energy also provides great pearls of wisdom which allow us to mature and evolve.

However, even though both people contribute to the quality of the energy that flows between them, most times, they are unaware of this factor. I will further add, we either have the appropriate relationship with things or we have an inappropriate relationship with things. These things may include money or food or time or people. This also applies to the relationship we have with ourselves, our families, our jobs, our spiritual practice, authority figures, the animal kingdom, Mother Nature, the plant kingdom, our health, and even our exercise or lack of it. Keep in mind the energy principle which states that the universe wants all events from our past and present to be brought to their highest vibrational state for all concerned. This is enlightenment, maturity, and evolution for all sentient beings, so we can change the energy between us and other people and other things.

Where there is wisdom, peace, and higher vibration energy between two beings, there is harmony, evolution, and the appropriate relationship with one another. Learning the language of energy and how the universe works is one of the key elements to navigate our energy and our life's journey in a more wisdom-filled and empowering way. If we want to understand the universe and its principles, we will need to understand energy and the symbolic representation of energy. As my teachers would say, there is gaining of wisdom or there is gaining of nothing.

Respective to energetic boundaries, we will find a world of energy that surrounds us, mostly consisting of the energy we put out and the energy others around us send out. There is also an energy chord between us and everything we interact with. The higher wisdom that my elders taught me was to provide these energy chords with mindful and transforming energy. This can help us bring in qualities, vibrations, frequencies, and light that can clean our aura and the energy that permeates around our relationships. This promotes vitality and helps generate our actions to be more in line with our great purpose and not our past reactive behaviors, which keep us in a lower vibration.

What do I mean by *energetic boundaries?* This describes the subtle energy between us and everything we encounter. We can change that subtle energy into more comfortable energy for all concerned. We can also learn to advocate for ourselves and others without stress. The advance techniques regarding changing the energy between us and another person involve an invocation to learn how to apply a different and better energy so we all evolve and feel better within a relationship. The higher aspect of this is we can become aware that we can transform the energy that is around us. The universe will help us because of the golden rule of the universe: all energies must be brought to their highest levels of maturity and quality. How can we do this and what methods can we apply? My native stories tell us the following.

We can work with our energetic resources to clear and transform energy. Our energetic resources include our higher self, our guides, our spirit helpers, our teachers in spirit, and even our ancestors in the energy world. We access these energetic resources by using an energetic narrative that can transmute the stressful and depleting energy to higher quality energy.

Here is a good example: I remember many years ago, a woman came to free Friday night meditation. Afterward, she proceeded to badger me and was very demanding, stating she would not leave until she spoke to me. And that is the key: she wanted to speak *to* me, not *with* me. She spent about ten minutes complaining about almost everything, including that our facilities needed carpeting for meditation, we needed bigger windows to see outside, and we needed special T-shirts for all the volunteers. While she was talking, I began to ask my spirit guides with my internal voice: *Why is she here?* The answer was not only funny but very insightful to me. My spirit guides said, "Billie Topa Tate, sometimes it's not about you."

Internally, I started laughing because my mind was focused on how this relates to me, but truly it was not about me. Instead, it was about the vibration between her and me and how we contributed to the energy between us.

I immediately started asking for an adjustment of energy between us. First, I needed to awaken her to the awareness that she may have a pattern of being pessimistic and judgmental. I invoked my spirit guides to fill her and the energy between us with a want and desire for peace, respect, honor, and the important question of what was the real purpose of the interaction. After about five minutes, she stopped, became quiet, and then started to softly shed tears that rolled down her face very much like the beginnings of a quiet rainfall. She looked at me and said, "I apologize. I realized just now on how I was sounding and I feel sad and angry at the same time that I was telling you how to run your meditation."

Before I could say anything, she rushed out the door, not giving me a chance to respond. I knew that she was experiencing a shift of energy that promoted an awakened state of mind. I also knew it was important for me to ask for her personal guides to continue to help her.

I wrote the enclosed energetic narrative to help support a healing process, as well as to begin the adjustment of energy. This is what my spirit guides meant by saying that sometimes it's not about you.

The following invocation can be used to develop healthy energetic boundaries with people, situations, past or present, and also help provide wonderful insights to wisely advocate for yourself. The following invocation is to be read before sleep time every night. It is more powerful to read it out loud. Please keep a journal of signification dreams so you can review your wonderful progress. You will know what a significant dream is because it will stand out and you will have a deep knowing that it is associated with what you are working on. Sometimes you will see events within your dreams that have deep connections with your past lifetimes. How do we know certain dreams are related to our past life? The energy around the dream will have great depths to it and you will have a deep knowing that it is a past life you are viewing. Another way of knowing the dream was a past life event is the memory of it upon rising from sleep. You will remember it when you awaken from your dream, as it will have some episodic events within the dream. This is your spirit's way of helping you remember certain parts of your dream.

I always recommend keeping a journal for your insights and also a few notes about your dreams. This will help you connect with certain patterns within your dreams and also provide wonderful insights for resolution from your invocation.

Invocation for Setting Energetic Boundaries

By the power of my good merits, I invoke my virtuous helpers, my virtuous teachers in spirit, my personal inner plane helpers, the angels and helpers of setting healthy energetic boundaries, the divine helpers of safety, and all the wonderful beings who assist me in virtuous ways. Please provide your divine intervention, divine guidance, divine mentorship, wonderful healing medicine, and resolution energy to the following request.

Secure that my energy field contributes in wisdom-filled ways to the energy around me and all the energy that influences me and influences others with peaceful energy. Secure that my energy influences all situations, people, events with the virtues of enlightenment and compassion. Transform all energy around me to do no harm but rather advocate peace and a willingness to honor and respect everything here and now and from this day forward at all energy levels. Transform harmful energy in a five-hundred foot circumference around me to peace, virtuous wisdom, and virtuous awareness. When I encounter harmful energy, halt that energy immediately and transform it into divine light and virtuous actions. Remove any and all hidden agendas from people and other forces which may impact my well-being and the well-being of others around me, physically, emotionally, mentally, spiritually, and at all other levels, here and now and from this day forward. Thank you and please provide healing medicine during our sleep time so we can all evolve and follow the integrity of our virtuous great purpose. In full faith, so be it now, thank you.

If there are chronic people that are giving you a hard time, for example at work, you can ask that they be kept virtuously busy and, through this request, that they will evolve and stop their harsh behavior. However, keep in mind that there is a life lesson for you in this situation, and ask your divine helpers to provide you with that insight during your sleep time.

Please add this short narrative to help this situation:

Secure that I receive virtuous mentoring for any life lessons there are for me in this situation. Also, secure virtuous mentoring for any life lessons there are for anyone who is involved with me for the purpose of gaining virtuous wisdom and wonderful evolution for our life's journey. Also, keep all harmful people virtuously busy so they have no time to even send harmful energy my way. Here and now and from this day forward, physically, mentally, emotionally, and at all other energy levels. In full faith, so be it now, thank you.

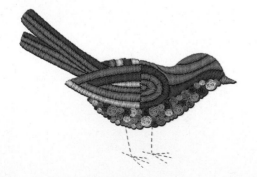

DEVELOP INTUITION

Everything starts with you. Are you ready to explore your intuition? What is intuition anyway? Intuition is often defined as the ability to understand something immediately without the need for conscious reasoning. Psychic abilities are different than intuition. However, both are very important to have available to us. Intuition and psychic abilities go hand in hand. The difference between intuition and psychic abilities is that intuition provides a deeper, more accurate knowing about what we are focusing upon.

Psychic abilities have several components. One component is psychic hearing, which means you would have the ability to hear your spirit guides, just like you hear a person standing next to you providing accurate information or insights. Psychic touch is another component of psychic abilities, which means you would have the ability to touch an object and receive images and feelings from that object. Psychic sight is an additional psychic ability that enables you to see more subtle energy as well as your spirit helpers and angels.

All these abilities are exciting skills that add great value to making decisions, such as buying a house, buying a car, and even making decisions about whether or not to have a selective surgery, just to name a few examples.

In this chapter is an invocation that will assist you in developing the inner skill of intuition. Having intuition is your sovereign right and this powerful skill is always within you. As your intuition begins to develop, apply efforts to securing your accuracy by invoking for the information you receive to be accurate, precise, and correct. Ask your guides to remove anything you are receiving that is not accurate. Think of this request of removing inaccurate information as a filter to fine-tune your intuition.

What if you do not receive information right away? This is very common in the beginning. I recommend that you take a break, do a short meditation, take a nature walk (if possible), and then try again. These simple practices can reset your focus and balance emotions enough to receive good answers to your questions.

How can you know the difference between your intuition and inaccurate information? The mystical answer is when you are receiving accurate information, you will know it is true within every cell of your being and you will feel empowered by the information you receive.

How can you strengthen your intuition and make it more reliable and consistent? To strengthen your intuition, it is important to honor this innate ability by using it and then expressing gratitude to that part of your consciousness, thus engaging and developing a rapport with your intuition. To make it more reliable is to always apply a filter to your received information. This will be covered by the following invocation, but generally speaking, when you ask a question, also add that you only accept information that is accurate, precise, and correct. This will teach your mind to filter out information that is not accurate.

Develop Intuition Invocation

By the power of my good merits, I invoke for my personal angels and helpers. I invoke for the virtuous angels and helpers of intuition and my virtuous teachers in spirit. I also call upon the spirit helpers of receiving accurate, precise, and correct information from my intuition, my spirit guides and spirit helpers who assist in providing activation energy to my accurate and empowering intuition. I ask them to help me evolve and enlighten myself and use this wonderful tool to make good, wisdom-filled decisions within my daily activities. I also ask them to help provide wisdom-filled assistance to others. Here and now, and from this day forward, physically, mentally, emotionally, and at all other energy levels. So be it now, thank you.

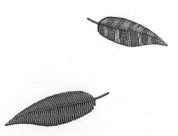

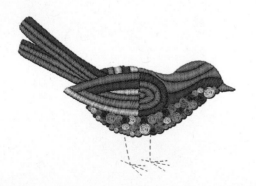

DEVELOP PSYCHIC ABILITIES

The most beautiful thing we can ever experience is the mysterious. Without exception, we all have psychic abilities. Yet, for most of us, they have not been nurtured, thus they lack development. But, what if I shared with you rarely known information and some insights regarding the development of your psychic abilities? Psychic abilities are, without a doubt, a very useful and wonderfully supportive energy tool for our daily activities. This chapter guides you to go beyond our ordinary awareness into the realms of the Place of Light and the Divine through the development of our psychic abilities.

We are all psychic. There are endless instances of mysterious spontaneous insight that we encounter in our daily lives. How important is it to have psychic abilities? The intuitive and psychic sense allow us to go beyond the normal mind and discover information that will help us in many good and empowering ways. This alone can be an important and motivating factor. We can also consider what great value our spirit helpers and other spirit guides can provide if we hear them clearly. It is our sovereign right to have all our psychic faculties available throughout our daily lives.

There are several psychic abilities we have and can develop. The psychic abilities of sight, hearing our spirit guides and knowing much-needed information, in my opinion, are the most important. The benefits of these resources aid us in making better wisdom-filled choices—for example, when you are trying to decide a major purchase, such as a house or car. This helps us to evolve and have a deep feeling of being wisely supported and assisted. When using the Psychic Abilities Sacred Invocation, encourage and acknowledge even the slightest of improvements. This helps create a deeper rapport with your awakened abilities and a deeper rapport with your angels and spirit guides. Also, as a point of reference, in the beginning, your angels and guides will communicate with you through a thought or a knowing that you receive within your mind. Say thank you when this happens so you can acknowledge your angels and spirit guides. As you progress, you will be able to hear your angels and your spirit guides. Always express gratitude when this happens, to secure a wonderful connection with them, and to demonstrate that you are evolving and using thoughts and emotions that truly matter regarding your evolution.

Developing Our Psychic Abilities Invocation

By the power of my good merits, I invoke my wisdom self, the shaman within me, the angels and spirit guides who assist in developing my wisdom-filled psychic abilities, my personal spirit guides, my personal angels, my virtuous teachers in spirit, and all the wonderful beings who assist me in virtuous ways.

I thank you for your guidance, intervention, mentorship, healing qualities, wisdom, and resolution energies for the following request:

Please secure that my psychic abilities develop in an empowering way for the purpose of assisting me in making wise decisions. Help me enhance and develop my psychic abilities of insight, information, and hearing my guides who can assist me in virtuous ways. Secure the help I need to also assist others to become more wise about their life journeys. Here and now, and from this day forward, physically, mentally, emotionally, and at all other energy levels. In full faith, so be it now, thank you.

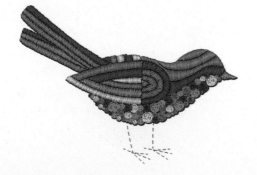

THE BATHING OF LIGHT

Wouldn't it be wonderful if we all started every year with a beautifully clean, lighter-than-air energy field, leaving behind everything but the wisdom for our healing and evolution? Well, this is entirely possible.

In the Apache tradition, every year, in January, it is customary to begin the year with an energetic cleansing ceremony called the Bathing of Light. This is facilitated for each family member. It is similar to the sunlight during the day; we are bathed in sunlight that lifts our spirit and provides vitality.

The ceremony cleanses body, mind, and spirit from all the stress and constrictive energy of the previous year. This practice refreshes and rebalances the body, mind, and spirit with a beautiful cleansing from plants harvested from a sacred harvest. Vibrant flowers are also used to bless the body, mind, and spirit. Lastly, but just as important, is a Bathing of Light sequence where a sphere of light bathes the body, mind, and spirit with healing light. This removes the trauma from the previous year, leaving only the wisdom of each event for our evolution. It is great way to start a new year.

Of course, it would be impossible to do this ceremony for you within this book. However, since energy crosses the span of time and space, powerful words can channel a wonderful request for energy cleansing through a special Bathing of Light invocation, found in this chapter. As with all requests, the more often we use the invocation, the more particles of light will be provided each time, and the more aware you will become of the healing light you are receiving.

Even though the Bathing of Light is used during the first month of the year, I encourage you to use this invocation anytime you feel you need a good energy cleanse and continue to use it until you feel balanced and cleansed. I would also recommend you keep a journal of all your insights and sensations to help you receive optimal results. The great mysteries of healing light—combined with your heartfelt desire to clear away a trauma, transcend all constrictive energy, and secure the wisdom of the event—can truly provide a great number of benefits.

Please read this invocation out loud with mindful focus before your sleep time. It is always best to be in the comfort of your bed so you can gently drift into sleep to receive a healing, cleansing Bathing of Light.

The Bathing of Light Invocation

By the power of my good merits, I invoke the Bathing of Healing Light angels and helpers, my personal spirit guides, my personal angels, the angels and helpers that remove trauma from our energy field at all levels, the plant medicine kingdom, the flower kingdom, the place of healing light kingdom, and all the wonderful spirit helpers who assist me in wonderful and virtuous ways. I thank all these kingdoms for helping me and my family. I am grateful for your assistance. Please provide your intervention, guidance, mentorship, healing energies, wisdom, and resolution energy to the following requests:

During my sleep time, I am super conductive and I am super receptive to receiving a bathing of healing light for my physical, mental, emotional, and spiritual parts of me, here and now and from this day forward. During my sleep time, please cleanse my energy field at all levels from all the traumas and stressful situations I have experienced from the time of my birth in this lifetime all the way up to this very day. Take these traumas and stressful situations to receive medical care in the spirit world, never to return to me, and be totally transformed into divine light, permanently. Please fill the void from which all was removed with a great sense of safety, peace, wisdom, and enlightenment. I ask that my aura feel lighter than air so I feel a great uplifting energy in my heart and spirit.

Please bless my energy field at all levels with divine light throughout my sleep time. Bathe my energy field in healing light and fill me with a great sense of harmony and divine love for myself and others. I ask that my aura feel healthy so I feel a great lifting in my heart and spirit. I thank you for the blessings that are on their way to me, here and now, and from this day forward, physically, mentally, spiritually, emotionally, and at all other levels. In full faith, so be it now, thank you.

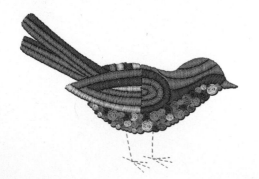

Invocations

REMOVING LONELINESS

Friendship most certainly supports, nourishes, and sustains us. Periods of isolation, especially during the COVID-19 pandemic, made it abundantly clear how much we mean to each other. Loneliness swept the world even more than before. Keeping in mind that everything is energy first and foremost, there is a refreshing aspect to asking our spirit guides to help us spark purpose and also spark empowering human connections. It's also helpful for working on our own patterns that may cause us to feel a sense of loneliness.

At the end of this chapter is an invocation that will help us work on underlining proclivities which may cause us to be lonely, but also help us to open empowering doors of opportunity to meet wonderful people. The invocation will also help to transform all blocks and obstacles to opening up our community for new circles of great friendships.

Please read this invocation at bedtime and also in the morning to help facilitate a faster change of energy. I recommend keeping a journal to track your progress and use meditation on a daily basis to be guided by higher thought. Continue reading the invocation nightly until the energy of loneliness has completely disappeared.

Removing Loneliness Invocation

By the power of my good merits, I invoke the virtuous angels and helpers of empowering relationships, the virtuous helpers of healing the emotions of the heart, the angels, and the helpers of releasing and clearing fears and anxieties.

Please remove my loneliness, my despair, and lift my unawareness of what I need to do, think, and feel in order to step into healing myself and feeling confident about myself. Please dismantle my anxieties, my fears, and my loneliness. Extract them from my energy field and my consciousness and take them to receive medical care in the spiritual world, never to return to me in any way, shape, or form, and transform them into divine light permanently. Fill the void from which they were removed with a great sense of purpose, healthy vitality, a great excitement for my future, and wonderful wisdom about my wellness and how I can participate in my wellness.

Remove the trauma within my energy field and consciousness that has been with me since the time of my birth. Take it to receive medical care in the spiritual world, transform it into divine light, and fill the void from which it was removed with a great sense of safety physically, mentally, emotionally, and at all other energy levels. Here and now, and from this day forward. In full faith, so be it now, thank you.

INVITING NEW AND BEAUTIFUL RELATIONSHIPS

People often think having a wonderful relationship is a mystery or maybe it just happens to other people and not them. Wouldn't it be interesting to find out there is an energetic science to relationships, as well as creating beautiful relationships that bring out the best in us and also bring out the best in our partner? Did you know that relationships are the bases of all we interact with? Yes, we have relationships with trees, plants, animals, water, crystals, family, co-workers, friends, and of course, the most important relationship, which is the relationship we have with ourself. The relationship we have with ourselves is the beacon of light that brings forth energy to us. And the symbolic aspect of relationships transcribes itself into the magic word *enlightenment*.

Relationships are the mystical journeys we take to learn how to truly interact with ourself and all the other kingdoms, and that includes the angelic kingdom and our spirit helpers. As we evolve from each relationship, we become mindful and awake to the idea that possibly we can navigate new energy to our future relationships, thus creating something new, wonderful, and much better than the past.

This chapter not only helps us to understand the energetic science of how to invite beautiful relationships to us, but also how to utilize powerful techniques that can help guide us to our happiness and wellness within relationships. Included within this chapter is a special relationship invocation to be read on a daily basis, every night at bedtime. Relaxing and drifting into sleep with these wonderful sacred intentions is the best way to connect with a very powerful aspect of our mind, as well as to gain the assistance of our spirit helpers and angels.

Before using the relationship invocation, it is important to define your personal concerns and/or fears regarding relationships. Please list them out on a piece of paper so you can insert them into the relationship invocation. During my medicine woman training, my teacher said you cannot change what you cannot see. It is important to clarify what your personal concerns and/or fears regarding relationships are, so these energies can be transformed into energies of happiness and wellness. It is always helpful to use a short meditation before creating your list so you are guided by higher thought and receive the assistance of your angels and spirit guides. After the meditation, simply write down a list of your fears or concerns about relationships. A good example of fears or concerns about relationships would be as follows: *No one out there will ever understand me, or, Most men cannot be trusted.* It might take a few days to complete your list, so take your time. Then insert all your fears and concerns into the relationship invocation and read it every night. Our goal is to not only clear out our fears and concerns but also re-invent our perspectives regarding relationships, as well as infuse our energy field with new thoughts and feelings that truly matter, hence, navigating new, fresh wisdom energy into our life. Our guides and personal angels will help us via the invocation.

Lastly, look at the things that have happened to you as a lifeway door to release something old which will then empower you with wisdom to help you utilize evolved energy and powerful words to move you forward with wisdom and peace.

Inviting New Beautiful Relationships Invocation

By the power of my good merits, I invoke for my virtuous spirit helpers and the angels of virtuous relationships—as well as my personal guides, personal helpers, personal angels, my virtuous family and ancestors in the energy world—to provide virtuous intervention, guidance, virtuous mentorship, healing energies, wisdom, and resolution energy to the following request.

Please provide healing energy to my personal fears and concerns regarding relationships. Here is my list (place your list here). Transform these fears and concerns into virtuous uplifting insights and wonderful empowering energy for me, so that I can accept my own goodness and allow empowering people to come into my life. I ask for these relationships to bring out the best in me and that I bring out the best in them.

If applicable you can include the following: Secure a wonderful relationship for me that will bring forth a wonderful life partner that is compassionate, has patience, wellness in body, mind, and spirit. Let us both bring out the best in each other in very empowering ways. Also, please virtuously mentor me to accept the goodness other people wish to give me and that I allow for empowering energy and people to come into my life.

Here and now and from this day forward, physically, mentally, emotionally, and at all other levels. In full faith, so be it now, thank you.

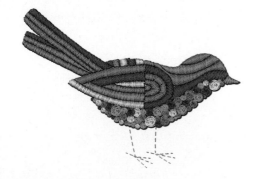

HARMONY AT WORK AND REMOVING BULLY ENERGY

Bullies are not always limited to our school playground. Bullies can roam our offices and can be found in lunchrooms and boardrooms. They don't steal your lunch but they can certainly make your work life very uncomfortable and stressful. Whether the bully is a boss or a co-worker, or whether you are the target of verbal abuse, manipulation, or deliberate humiliation, the enclosed invocation can help dismantle this type of behavior within the structure of any bully dynamic and also work on any limited qualities within yourself to set boundaries, advocate for yourself, and learn how to transform bully energy in any area of your life into honor and respect and fairness. Also, this invocation will help you be guided to advocate for yourself, and have courage to speak to authorities who will listen and help you. I also recommend that you take time to do some meditation regarding other wellness skills to help this situation be transformed into one of safety and maturity. The invocation is certainly a place to start when defending yourself during difficult times with bullies. Also, this invocation will help you energetically learn assertiveness, which is a style of communication that empowers us to speak out and stand up for ourselves in clear, respectful, but knowledgeable ways. It allows for the confident expression of your needs and feelings. Advocating for ourselves is a stepping stone to feeling empowered within our own mind as well as at work and at home. Helping us to send the message: this is how I want to be treated while respecting other people's rights and opinions as well.

Removing Bully Energy Invocation

By the power of my good merits, I invoke for my divine helpers, angels of compassion, the angels and helpers of healing emotionally harmful energy, the angels and helpers of removing bully energy at all levels, the angels and helpers of patience and awareness.

Please provide your intervention, guidance, mentorship, healing energies, wisdom, and resolution energy to the following situations.

Dismantle any and all bully energy toward me and others, deactivate aggressive actions and any aggressive thoughts, and transform them into kindness, compassion, peaceful cooperation, honor, respect, and fairness. Pick up all harmful energies within all individuals I work with that have bully energy, be they within my workplace, home, friendships, school activities, and social circles. Secure the energy of honor and respect and peaceful harmony between me and everyone, especially incorporated into the bully I encounter today and for the next seventy-two hours, and any energy or force that tries to cause harm at any level to be picked up and taken for healing in the spirit world, totally transformed into divine light permanently. Secure that all bullies that are around me be halted and kept virtuously busy, and secure they mature, heal, and evolve. Secure to keep them away from me and keep them away from working with me. Virtuously mentor me to be wisely assertive and help me to improve my communication skills. I will face problems and/or conflicts with poise and a clearer head so I can make wise decisions.

Virtuously mentor me to wisely advocate for myself. Also, by the power of my good merits, secure that all authority figures see any and all bully energy and stop it immediately and administer consequences to secure a safe and respectful workspace for me and all other people surrounding the situation. Secure that others within my workspace stand together to dismantle bully energy and let peace, respect, and honor prevail. Also, halt all bully energy at all levels and provide healing medicine to the bully energy until it transforms into peace, honor, and harmony at all energy levels. Here and now and from this day forward, physically, mentally, emotionally, and at all other energy levels.

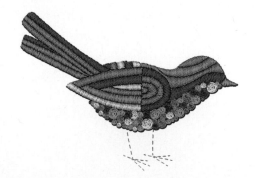

Invocations

CLEARING NEIGHBORHOODS OF NEGATIVE ENERGY

If we go back far enough in time, we can see the significance of energy within ancient villages that promoted creativity, innovation, and vitality. Our neighborhoods are most certainly influenced by various qualities of energy which can promote wisdom, awareness, evolution, safety, and wellness at all energy levels. The contribution of evolved energies allows for higher mature energies within our neighborhoods that lift our spirit. Therefore, the same stands true for negative energy which can also influence our neighborhoods with depression, unsafe conditions, and so much more. The Plains American Indians shared their wisdom with the European settlers about how to keep harmony with nature and create communities that would thrive. This chapter is about how to apply these timeless techniques to create safer communities and lift the spirit of our neighborhoods where we live and work.

You will learn how to administer qualities of energy that promote safety, wisdom, and other benefits, thus harnessing wonderful qualities of peace for all of us to thrive and be safe in our neighborhoods. We are all entitled to live in safety, peace, and wisdom. Our neighborhoods are places where there are so many energies, such as the energy of the region, the energy of each person that walks the neighborhood, also the energetic history of the neighborhood. The following story demonstrates the significance of a written invocation to direct healing energy toward our neighborhood.

I was taking my nephew home from a school meeting; he was talking to a new boy in his class and this boy said his mother was running very late. I spoke to her on the telephone and said I would be happy to drive him home. She said that they lived far away, and she was driving a company bus which was running late and would greatly appreciate me giving her son a ride home. I proceeded to travel to their neighborhood and, yes, it was a great distance. I observed the town was filled with drug addicts and gangsters throughout the streets and even the air was thick with violence. I knew at that time the universe guided me to give this boy a ride home so I could help clear the energy of the neighborhood. As soon as I dropped the boy off at his home safely, I composed and used an invocation to clear the energy of the neighborhood and continued to do so for the rest of the week. The following week I saw the boy again and, to my surprise, he was hoping I could give him a ride home as his mother was again going to be very late picking him up. As we arrived in his neighborhood, I was very surprised at the significant difference regarding the energy. The foggy dark energy was lifted. The gangsters and drug addicts were gone, and the energy felt very nice. The boy mentioned that for the past week the neighborhood had been so very quiet and even the mayor commented on how peaceful the small town was. This is a great verification that, as humans, we can be conduits of higher quality energy to transform the energy and lift the spirit of a region of land, keeping in mind that our spirit helpers and angels will help to clear out lower vibration energies because they want to provide healing medicine to harmful energies for evolution and healing, thus promoting a higher vibrational state for the area.

Enclosed is the invocation to clear your neighborhood of harmful energy. Please read it out loud on a daily basis for at least three months and then as needed. While reading this invocation, see your neighborhood or the neighborhood where you work within your mind. As the energy begins to change within your neighborhood, your neighbors might be open to the idea of reading the invocation as a group effort. Please provide them with a copy of this invocation. The rationale is there is power in the amount of people who read this invocation.

Please read the following invocation every night until you feel your request has been completed. Also, while you are reading this invocation, please visualize brilliant bright light in every aspect of the neighborhood. If you have difficulty visualizing, just read the invocation and say out loud, "My neighborhood is being filled with brilliant bright light."

Invocation to Clear Stressful and Negative Energy from Our Neighborhood

By the power of my good merits, I invoke for the spiritual medics to pick up all non-virtuous forces, all mental illness forces, all non-virtuous entities, all mental illness entities from people, noxious energies, and other planes of existence that have affected my neighborhood for the past seventy-two hours and have the medics take them to receive medical care in the entities' world never to return, and fill the void from which they were removed with divine light, divine love, divine peace, and virtuous uplifting wisdom for my neighborhood, here and now and from this day forward, physically, mentally, emotionally, and at all other levels.

Lift harmful energy off of each person that walks my neighborhood here and now and from this day forward and fill each person with virtuous energy; also lift the harmful energetic history off the neighborhood's region of land and replace it with divine peace. Whatever trauma this neighborhood has experienced for the past fifty years, remove the trauma, take all of it to receive medical care in the energy world, and fill the void from which it was removed with divine peace, kindness, and the will to do good.

Influence this neighborhood with harmony, and a general sense of divineness and well-being for all.

Also, secure virtuous energy within this neighborhood and secure that all people and energies that contribute to disharmony within my neighborhood be kept virtuously busy so they have no time to even think about doing any harmful acts. I have sovereignty within this neighborhood, because this neighborhood deserves to experience and have divine light, divine peace, and divine healing energy. Here and now and from this day forward, physically, emotionally, mentally, and at all other energy levels.

In full faith, so be it now, thank you.

Invocations

REMOVING NIGHTMARES

We can all benefit from a restful and rejuvenating sleep. Waking up refreshed and having a great sense of balance can boost our day with joy, zest, and liveliness. Unfortunately, there are adults, children, and even our pets, who do not experience and enjoy good-quality restful sleep. But, what if you can change all that? Suppose I were to tell you that you have living rights in your dream time? That's correct, you have dominion and sovereignty over your space and time within your dreams, but if you are not aware you have it, how can you take any amount of control of the quality of your dreams? My native traditions teach us that dreams are a training ground on how to navigate our energy.

Living rights within your dream time means you can remove any and all energies from your dreams that are stressful and harmful. You can also ask for your spirit helpers and your personal angels to transform the quality of your dreams to peaceful and wisdom-filled. Using the invocation within this chapter will help you do just that.

Removing nightmares and stressful sleep is very important for our vitality and our general well-being that affect our immune system, brain function, and healing.

The sleep realm is the more subtle realm of energy with lots of different energy levels, but within all those realms in dream time, you have sovereignty. But what does that mean? It means that no one has the right to harass you in dream time. So, if that is true, then why do we have nightmares or obscure dreams? Think of it this way: when you get into your car, you can go to different neighborhoods and all those different neighborhoods are not the same. What separates them is the quality of energy and the quality of people and spirits that live within that energy. Depending upon what you are working on within your life's journey to bring it to a more peaceful and evolved level, you could end up in dreams that are stressful. An example of this would be, possibly you are learning how to set boundaries, so your dreams may take you to places where you are harassed, chased, or generally bullied by people or entities. Until you figure out to set those boundaries, bring bright light into those situations, and also ask for your guides to pick up all the not-so-nice things and people within your dreams, you will continue to experience unsettling dreams. Our guides, angels, and helpers are happy to help us and will do so through our request within the enclosed invocation. We can also use our dreams to gain insight about things in our life, as well as request to receive healing and virtuous mentoring within our dreams.

In general, we are all using dream time to work things out, build our strengths, understand and transform our weaknesses, learn how to wisely stand in our power, and, most of all, mature, which is another word for enlightenment. Why is it important to use dreams and sleep wisely? So our sleep can add great value to our daily activities. In my mystical training, this is called *tending the energy of our energy field*. We cultivate the energy of our dreams to become enlightened and mindfully navigate our energy.

Enclosed within this chapter is a dream time invocation that removes nightmares and obscure dreams and promotes better dream time and restful sleep. Please use this dream time invocation for yourself, your children (especially if they have nightmares), your family and friends.

Removing Nightmares Invocation

By the power of my good merits, I invoke for my virtuous spirit guides, personal angels, the angels and helpers of removing harmful energies, and entities from my dream time and sleep time. Pick up all non-virtuous forces, all mental illness forces, all non-virtuous entities, and mental illness entities from people, noxious energies, and other planes of existence that may interfere with my restful sleep time and dream time to be taken to receive medical care in the spiritual realm. I wish for them to be transformed into divine peace, and to fill the void from which they were removed with virtuous peace for me and restful and empowering sleep. I invoke for my guides, angels, and divine helpers to surround me with virtuous energy throughout my sleep time.

In addition, whatever caused me to experience nightmares and unsettling dreams in the past, please have my divine helpers pick up these energies (wherever they are) and take them to the spirit world for healing medicine and fill the void with divine light for me. I further invoke for the qualities of high self-esteem, intrinsic self-worth, and have an excellent concept of virtuous self-talk for myself at all levels, here and now and from this day forward.

Also, I request to feel so wonderfully safe within my sleep and dream time, and, that upon rising, I feel refreshed and well-rested, physically, mentally, emotionally, and at all other energy levels. Here and now and from this day forward. In full faith, so be it now, thank you.

Removing Nightmares for Someone Else

By the power of my good merits, I invoke for my virtuous spirit guides, personal angels, the angels and helpers of removing harmful energies, entities from dream time and sleep time, the angels and divine helpers of divine light and divine peace, and all the virtuous helpers who assist me in virtuous ways. Please pick up all non-virtuous forces, all mental illness forces, all non-virtuous entities and mental illness entities from people, noxious energies, and other planes of existence that may interfere with (person's name) restful sleep time and dream time. Take all these interfering and stressful energies and forces to receive medical care in the spiritual realm and totally transform them into divine peace and fill the void from which they were removed with virtuous peace for (person's name here) and restful and empowering sleep. Here and now and from this day forward, at all energy levels. I invoke for my guides, angels and divine helpers to surround (person's name) with virtuous energy, starting now and for the next twenty-four hours) at all energy levels.

In addition, whatever caused (person's name) to experience nightmares in the past, please have my divine helpers pick up these energies and take them to the spirit world for healing medicine and fill the void with divine light for (say the person's name here). I further invoke for the qualities of high self-esteem, intrinsic self-worth, and have an excellent concept of virtuous self-talk for myself at all levels, here and now and from this day forward.

I request (person's name) to feel so wonderfully safe within their sleep and dream time, and upon rising, feel refreshed and well rested, physically, mentally, emotionally and at all other energy levels. Here and now and from this day forward. In full faith, so be it now, thank you.

OUR LOVED ONES IN THE SPIRIT WORLD

The world of spirit and the passing of our loved ones to the other side is the realm of endless experiences of the heart, but also takes our consciousness on a soulful journey of compelling and embracing mystical questions. We most certainly are never the same after experiencing the loss of a loved one. This chapter shares insight regarding the spirit voyage of our loved ones who have died and carries healing medicine for our hearts, as well as the great potential of being able to connect with them on the other side.

The passing of a loved one is a sacred journey indeed, not only for our loved one who has died, but also an awakening for the people who were connected to them. By this I mean, the sacred journey for us is more than just saying goodbye to a loved one in the physical and emotional sense.

Our loved one can be a companion animal or a human being; the heart sings the same song of questions, inquiries, expressed desires, contemplations, and even visions from the other side. When I lost a loved one and they transitioned to the spirit world, I was confronted with a cascade of contemplations, occurrences, happenings, and phenomena. In general, we may even experience a set of circumstances that teach us a valuable lesson regarding our own life. My mother taught me that when you first hear about someone dying, it is important to take a moment to send a loving thought of peace to that person and their family—but, also, to take a moment for ourselves to be grateful for our own life and our sacred journey, to honor and to respect this time we have here on Mother Earth. My mother (Mama Little Wolf) also taught us that when we hear about an accident, in addition to saying a prayer for all the people involved, deeply consider this information regarding the accident as a possible mystical message for us to take extra care within our journey.

Did you know that our loved ones on the other side retain the memory of their physical body, but their vibration is very different when they enter the spirit world? When we let go of the physical body and enter the spirit world, our vibration is more subtle and we carry all our regrets, thoughts, beliefs, and traumas, which take time in the spirit world to heal. When our regrets, thoughts, beliefs, traumas, and events begin the process of healing, the end result is the appearance of the energy field becoming lighter and brighter. So, when our loved ones visit us in dream time, their aura appears brighter and pure. To share some information regarding this point: Several years ago, I saw a dear friend in my dream time after he had passed away. I went to hug him, and he projected himself backwards and sent me a mind message that his vibration was so different from mine and because he was in the process of healing himself, I couldn't hug him as he needed to safeguard his vibration. He also communicated, he was still working with his inner plane helpers to learn more about where he was, as well as communicating to me that he was diligently working on learning how to maintain the vibration of peace. Later I found this information very helpful because every emotion and thought they experience can shift their energy into lower realms or higher realms. He also sent me a mind message that he was not even close to knowing how to cleanse his energy field and maintain the quality of peace within his energy field consistently. This is important to them because if they have a harmful or stressful thought, this changes the vibration of their energy field. The same holds true for us here on Mother Earth as well. When we are angry and agitated, we encounter situations, people, and events that create the same anger and agitation or more—unless we stop and use our energy tools, such as our invocations, meditation, and other energy-cleansing techniques which bring our energy field back into a vibration of harmony.

My teacher said that if you can navigate your energy field in dream time with wisdom, you will wisely navigate your life's journey here on earth.

People often ask the question, why hasn't my loved one come to see me in dream time? There are many reasons; one reason is we may still be in deep grief and their appearance in our dream time may relaunch deeper stress for us. The divine helpers who are helping our loved ones on the other side will ask them to wait until the grieving process is slightly over to secure they will not relaunch a deep sadness, sorrow, or depression within us. I would also add that our loved ones very much want to see us right away, but sometimes the angels and divine helpers talk with our loved ones to work on themselves and heal a little bit more, before they visit us on earth. That does not necessarily mean our loved ones can't help us during the time of their training and learning; on the contrary, our loved ones receive training on how to help us on the earth. Our deceased loved ones often request to become our angels on our earth journey and help the world we know. Through this process they learn how to become the light as well as do their best to move more light into our lives.

I have learned to help my students have patience, especially if they have not seen their loved ones in dream time. However, I have also learned that we can ask, through an invocation, for permission to speak to our loved one within our dream time.

This invocation is to be read before sleep time and provides a beautiful energy bridge during dream time. This bridge has a great potential to establish a connection with our loved ones on the other side. However, keep in mind, this may take time to allow us to speak with our deceased loved ones and, of course, we need to respect this wisdom. The universe and the Creator have reasons we may not totally understand; however, we can still ask to speak with our deceased loved ones and inquire about them. Sometimes, they are still learning various qualities of wisdom to help us or they may be healing specific things within themselves, or they may be working with other loved ones who need their immediate help. Within all these reasons, we need to have patience and ask questions during our meditations to understand more about what we do not know regarding our loved one in the energy world.

Enclosed are two invocations. The first invocation is to help receive additional mentoring to understand the inner workings of the spirit world. The second invocation is to help us talk with our loved ones on the other side. Both invocations can provide comfort and insight.

Invocation to Work with Virtuous Teachers

By the power of my good merits, I invoke for my virtuous higher self, my virtuous teachers in spirit, the angels of wisdom, and the angels of virtuous mentoring. Please provide your wonderful intervention, divine guidance, and virtuous healing energy for the following request. I request that my virtuous teachers in spirit during my sleep time provide me with wonderful wisdom and virtuous wisdom training for the purpose of developing and evolving myself, especially to understand how my loved one who passed over is doing (place name here). I wish to use this wonderful wisdom to help heal myself and provide compassionate healing for others, be they animals, plants, or humans. Here and now and from this day forward, physically, mentally, emotionally, and at all other energy levels. In full faith, so be it now, thank you.

Invocation to Speak to Our Loved Ones in the Energy World

By the power of my good merits, I ask for the angels who are helping my loved one who transitioned recently, my virtuous angels, and all the virtuous helpers who assist me in good and virtuous ways. Please bless (place the name of person who has transitioned) and myself with peace, divine love, and divine light, and with the qualities of joyful wisdom to help us to be able to talk to each other for the purpose of comforting each other and providing both of us healing energy. Please help transform our grief into virtuous empowering energy for both of us. Please create a wonderful space within my dream time for the both of us to comfort each other in peaceful ways. I invoke that virtuous angels gather around us and bless us with healing energy. I ask that both my loved one (place name here) and myself, during dream time, cross the bridge of light to speak to each other and comfort each other. I ask this by the power of my good merits. I also ask for my virtuous helpers to help (place the name of person who transitioned) and me through these difficult times, and help us to be able to talk to each other for the purpose of healing our grief in virtuous ways. Thank you so much. Please bless me and my loved one with wonderful empowering dream time and always surround us both with divine love and divine light. In full faith, so be it now. Thank you for your divine help and thank you for helping me visit with my loved one. In full faith, so be it now, thank you.

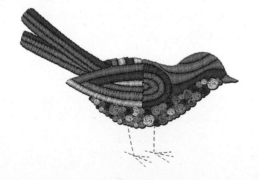

SAFE TRAVEL

When we use our travel invocations, we transform the energy around us as a result, we receive help from the energy world, thereupon developing a kinship with the natural world, and remember that we can walk with the powerful assistance of the Creator's helpers. As my teacher would say, words make worlds.

Did you know, in between us and our travel destination is mystical energy? Wouldn't it be wonderful if all our travels were filled with great timing, perfect weather, comfortable flights, and much more? If you are interested in navigating your travels with beautiful energy, you will love the travel invocations within this chapter. The navigation factor regarding travel is a concept that many people never truly become aware of. But, we can think of travel as a way of not only experiencing the journey and the destination, but also learning how to create energy for a great trip. The energy between us and our target destination is called mystical energy, which can be navigated. Travel energy is impacted by the regions of land and by the energy people and other living systems contribute. It's also impacted by how we contribute energy mindfully to our travel. All these energies combined can and do affect the quality of our travel. We often think travel is a movement of ever-present fixed objects, such as heavy traffic, airplane delays, auto accidents, drug infested area, weather conditions. Also, our destination point may have agitating energy, such as when we visit our family during the holidays and may not get along with a sibling or a parent. This chapter provides a travel invocation to influence all the energies of our travel. Since there are many different types of travel situations, I provide several written invocations to help these various types of travel situations.

Use the invocations within this chapter to create sacred time for yourself to pour good-quality energy into your travel journey. My grandfather said, when nothing is sacred almost anything can go wrong. I can hear my grandfather's voice as I write this sentence. When we connect with the land we are traveling and connecting with the energy we would like to experience, it is very much like sending a blessing to a very powerful person who you will be visiting and that person, in deep appreciation, sending a convoy of energy soldiers to secure your safe passage.

When we create and use a sacred invocation, especially reading the invocation out loud, we receive the attention of the universe and all our divine helpers who would like very much to help us. We are also adjusting our energy field to help navigate us in the direction we wish to travel and the quality of our journey. Many helpers in the energy world will be there to guide us.

During family trips, I can remember, after we were all packed, ready to go, my mother and father would gather us to sit within a spirit circle. This beautiful circle consisted of all members who were traveling and also some members that were staying behind. We would close our eyes and focus on our heart area and the top of our head. Our leaders would proceed with a beautiful ceremony. During the ceremony we were all blessed and cleansed with the traditional plants which were set afire within an abalone shell to produce the purification smoke. Our elders would cleanse our energy field with the dried plant smoke to release all negativity and fill our hearts with love and happiness. Each time, I would feel a wonderful sense of well-being, and the entire room was filled with peace, oneness, and healing energy. My grandfather shared how important the plants were for our well-being. The plants gift us with food, medicine, and ceremony. We would always thank the plants for helping us especially, during our prayers, songs, and ceremony.

Within our sacred energetic writings of invocations for a safe journey, we included the honoring of all of nature, because nature is the doorway to our wellness and helps support our travels. My grandfather would tell me that the plants and herbs are food for us, medicine for us, and help us in our ceremonies. He used to say, we cannot live without the plants and the trees, but…they can most certainly live without us; they have no dependencies upon the human kingdom. However, the Creator sent them here; they are here to help us. Grandfather used to say, one thousand eyes are watching us, not to judge us, but to gauge the level of self-awareness we demonstrate, for the purpose of establishing a connection and energy language with us. The one thousand eyes are the eyes of the plants, trees, nature spirits, and much more. The plants would help us and show us what to eat and show us what plants can heal us. The weather spirits would help support our journey and the spirit of the land would guide us.

Traveling for the tribal people had many mystical meanings and served various purposes, besides truly helping to create community among the people. The efforts of everyone helping each other is the nectar of spirit itself. There were also the sacred intentions of the elders and medicine people within the tribe. The bandanas that were worn around the forehead of native elders and medicine teachers were not just to keep the sweat away from the brow, but rather to place and anchor a small crystal on the area called the third eye. This enabled the medicine men and women and tribal leaders to see ethereal energy and allowed the ability to see land much farther away where the visible eye could not reach. This ethereal sight also enabled them to see the vitality of plants and many other things necessary for safe and healthy travel.

The elders and medicine men and women said an invocation to speak with the energies and energy helpers within the land that was targeted to travel to secure the cooperation of all the regions of land and all the energies and helpers within the land. I learned how to do this and used it when taking large groups on trips to regions of mountains and land. I would speak with the guardians of mountains, sacred places, and even before climbing difficult regions. The spirits of these places would always let me know when rain or hail was coming so I would have time to bring the people to safe areas.

Before we traveled—whether it was by car, plane or just visiting relatives in another city—we always took time to ask for wonderful energy, good experiences, a safe journey, and much more through our travel invocations.

You will find that, when the family reads these invocations as a group, more wonderful power is added to your request. Also, the words *thank you* at the end of the invocation are important to let your wonderful guides and divine helpers know that the invocation and request are completed.

The following are several different travel invocations, as there are many different situations when we travel. I have written several travel situations for you to use. Please read them out loud before you begin your travel.

The family vacation invocation should be read several months before the actual vacation. This will help build wonderful energy for safe travel but also harmony, peace, and comfortable travel. It is best to read out loud, but you can also read the sacred invocation and visualize all the qualities you requested while you are reading it.

Safe Family Vacation Travel Invocation

By the power of my good merits, I invoke for my personal guides and divine helpers, the wonderful spirit helpers for safe travel, the travel spirit guides of the regions I will be traveling, the plant medicine spirits of the regions respective to the areas my family will be traveling to and from, the weather angels, the divine helpers of safety, the divine helpers of protection, my virtuous teachers in spirit, and all the wonderful beings who assist me in wonderful and virtuous ways. Please provide your divine intervention, divine healing medicine, divine guidance, safety, and protection at all energy levels to the following request.

My family and I are going on a family vacation. We humbly request your assistance to secure that our vacation and our travel be filled with peace, joy, good timing, cooperation, harmony, and safety. Secure that our flight, our car, and everything we do be filled with divine light, virtuous joy, and safety. Let no accidents happen to us in a five hundred-foot circumference around us, physically, mentally, emotionally, and at all other energy levels. Secure that we enjoy our travel time and that our luggage and all our personal belongings arrive in excellent condition and on time with us, physically, emotionally, mentally, spiritually, and all other energy levels.

Secure that our finances will not be drained regarding our vacation and travel. Secure that everything at home is also protected. Secure that all companion animals, our home, our car, and our businesses be filled with your divine protection and divine virtuous energies.

Secure that our loved ones at home be filled with divine and virtuous energies and surrounded with harmony, peace, and safety, physically, emotionally, mentally, spiritually, and at all other energy levels, here and now and from this day forward.

Secure that everyone attending our family vacation utilize the energy of honor, respect, peace, happiness, and joyfully enjoy our family vacation. Secure everyone that is around us be filled with peaceful and respectful energy. Secure that everyone we interact with is kind, helpful, and supportive, and assist us to have beautiful, empowering, and joyful vacation and travel, physically, emotionally, mentally and at all other energy levels. And when we arrive back home, we will all take great joy that we traveled together for our family vacation. Here and now and from this day forward, in full faith, so be it now. Thank you.

Invocation Before You Drive Your Car

The following invocation I use daily before I drive anywhere, especially for my daily trips to my office. This only takes a few minutes and truly surrounds all who use this invocation with safety and protection. If possible, please read it out loud and visualize a beautiful sphere of light around you and your car as you read it.

By the power of my good merits, I invoke the angels and helpers of safety, the angels and helpers of protection, my virtuous divine helpers, my personal guides, my personal angels, and virtuous ancestors. Please provide your virtuous intervention, virtuous protection, virtuous guidance, and healing medicines to the following request.

Surround my car and all who are in my car with protection and safety from all harm, physically, mentally, emotionally, and at all energy levels. Secure that no accidents happen to me or around me and my vehicle in a five hundred-foot circumference around myself and my vehicle. Secure that all vehicle drivers that are in a five hundred-foot circumference around me practice safe and wisdom-filled driving. Also, that I practice safe and wisdom-filled driving so safety, wisdom, awareness, and patience be ever present within myself and all other drivers around me, physically, mentally, emotionally, and at all other levels, here and now and from this day forward. In full faith, so be it now, thank you.

Travel Invocation for Public Transportation

By the power of my good merits, I invoke the angels and helpers of transportation, the angels and helpers of safety, the angels of protection, my virtuous divine helpers, my personal guides, my personal angels, and virtuous ancestors. Please provide your virtuous intervention, virtuous protection, virtuous guidance, virtuous mentorship, virtuous resolution energy, and healing medicines to the following request.

I will be traveling on the bus and train today to arrive at work, safe and sound. Secure that my travel with public transportation today be filled with safety, peace, honor, respect, and divine light for not only myself, but all who enter this bus (or train). Totally transform my bus ride (or train ride) into the highest quality of peace, wisdom, consideration, and enlightenment for myself and everyone who travels on this public transportation today and for the life of the vehicle. Halt all violence and harmful energy and take it to receive medical care in the spiritual world and fill the void from which it was removed with divine and virtuous light—permanently. Here and now and from this day forward, physically, mentally, emotionally and at all other levels. In full faith, so be it now. Thank you.

I recommend that you read the invocations daily. Take a quiet moment and focus on your breath being in a state of peace. These energy tools work best when we mindfully move our focus into our sacred invocations.

In conclusion, please begin to read your travel invocation at least several weeks before you begin your journey. This preparation time is helpful so the universe can better prepare your wonderful travel and journey.

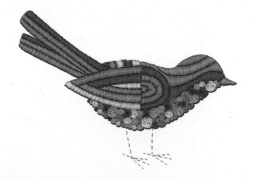

ACQUIRING ADVANCED FUTURE SKILLS

Words and breath are actually energy packets that influence our energy field and can alter our world, and create new endeavors for us or restrict us from our life's purpose. The rhythm of our breath is also a powerful tool; the mystical aspect of our breath is quite unique. My teacher taught me to observe the breath of people because our breath is much more unique that any fingerprint.

When we breathe in a shallow way, and in a stressful and restrictive manner, we are unintentionally sending a message to the universe that we are not entitled to a full breath of life. Many times, my teacher shared that most of us can demonstrate the breath of worry, the breath of anger, the breath of fear, the breath of frustration, the breath of loneliness, and even the breath of struggle. However, very few people can easily demonstrate the breath of peace, the breath of wisdom, or even the breath of ceremony.

The basic aspect of our breath vibrates at a rate that is more reactive and without mindfulness. However, as we progress, we use our breath in a positive and more evolved way, hence activating our evolution, knowledge, wisdom, and perspectives.

My teacher also said that our breath is a gift that was given to us to help us to not only live and enjoy our physical experience on this wonderful Mother Earth, but also to help us transform all things within us and around us. The breath generates power, purpose, and can very well manifest healing energies. The breath is a mystical tool and also an energy tool to disperse the most constrictive aspects of our past lives and even the traumas of this lifetime. According to my teacher, the Creator designed our blood cells to not only convert food into energy but aspects of our blood, such as the red blood cells to carry oxygen, serve as a function of providing energy—but what kind of energy? Depending upon the quality of our breath, we generate positive or negative energy. Also our blood cells can energetically activate our great purpose or activate our old proclivities and old patterns as a way of helping us evolve and mature.

I coined the phrase *wisdom logs*, or *wisdom sharing*, to define and categorize all my discussions with my teachers. During one of my teacher's wisdom sharings, he shared with me a very old story about the Creator regarding advanced forms of breath and how they can promote powerful energy for us. The Creator stated that the inner universe, which is our blood stream, holds a very interesting force and symbol of energy. The Creator, with infinite wisdom provided, this gift within our blood stream. My teacher said there are two very important energy molecules that ride on the red blood cells. I found this to be extremely useful and truly explained how mystical and unique our energy field truly is. I am sharing this information with you to help you access powerful ways of using your breath to launch good-quality energy within your aura and also your journey. One energy molecule which rides on the red blood cell carries all that is positive and the other one carries all that is negative. The different types of breath we utilize launch either the positive energy or the negative energy, and this happens all day long and also in the evening. In general, our breath is connected to the oxygen particles riding on the red blood cells. With our breath we launch either our great purpose or our restrictive patterns and traumas. Thus, we experience constrictive events and constrictive outcomes when we breathe in a constrictive manner because it launches the energetic molecule of our old unevolved patterns. We also can experience beautiful wisdom and healing resolution when we breathe expansively because this type of breath launches the positive energy molecules within our red blood cells and helps our actions be more in line with our wellness. Wouldn't it be interesting if we could use this knowledge to learn and practices breathing which is more in line with good health, prosperity, creativity, high self-esteem, and much more?

With this understanding, we can use the example of the medicine woman who often uses energetic narratives to invoke the assistance of our spirit guides to provide mentorship and specialized training during our sleep time, specifically for future skills, but also we can ask for help with current situations. Sacred invocations are often used to resolve old traumas from past lives, but they can also be used to receive wonderful training for future qualities that we may need for our journey here and now. In other words, the medicine woman brings the additional level of awareness to an already wonderful energy tool of invocation to start developing future skills to incorporate into her journey here and now. Of course, angels and divine helpers are more than willing to provide this type of wisdom to you as it serves as assistance to your evolution. Because this assistance is all about virtuous evolution, we can learn qualities that are filled with progress, advancement, and development. A perfect example of this is how the medicine woman would use sacred invocations to learn about future events that may be harmful to the tribal members and through her visions would recommend the tribe take up camp and move the entire village for safety reasons to another location. She would also need to learn how to direct the tribal members to a new location that was not only safe but also had all the necessary needs, such as fresh water, stable fruitful land, and possibly had plant-based medicines available for the tribal members. The medicine woman would use the invocations to learn how to make medicine from different varieties of plants and detect when storms would occur to direct the tribal members to take shelter and, at times, collect rainwater.

The medicine woman learned, through her sacred invocations, when to use sacred objects to connect to the Creator's powerful Place of Light. Wood that was struck by lightning was used to make talking sticks, shields, dream catchers, medicine staffs, journey staffs, sacred drums, and many other energy tools because we believe that wood which was struck by lightning was touched by the finger of God. The wood was then energized in a very sacred and powerful way. The medicine woman used sacred invocation to learn how to dry herbs while keeping their powerful medicine and so much more.

During my preliminary training with my teachers, I witnessed a very interesting and wisdom-filled endeavor from one of our elders who was assisting in a ceremony called the sweat lodge ceremony. The sweat lodge is a sacred ceremony reserved for indigenous members and by special invitation. My teacher was standing next to the fire keeper, who was tending the sacred fire. The fire keeper is an important part of the sweat lodge ceremony as he or she tends the fire with many prayers and heats up the stones that were gathered from the nearby river early that day (or sometimes the stones come from a family member who gathered them the previous day). These stones are to be used in the sweat lodge for our purification ceremony. Before we enter the lodge, the medicine man or medicine woman provides a pinch of tobacco to all the members and one by one they line up to stand in front of the fire, make a private prayer or a sacred intention for their time in the sweat lodge, and express a desire for their sweat lodge experience. The members then toss the tobacco into the fire. The participant proceeds to walk around the fire and then proceeds to approach the sweat lodge. Before entering the lodge, they say another private prayer, then send a prayer to Mother Earth, followed by a moment of peace to ask permission to come into the lodge, and then enters the sweat lodge. During the process of offering up the tobacco to the sacred fire and then walking around the fire, the medicine man or medicine woman observes how they approach the fire to make a prayer and then observes how each participant walks around the fire. The most interesting part of this observation was explained to me by my teacher. How the person approaches the fire, and then walks around the fire before entering the sweat lodge, shows the medicine man or medicine woman how they approach life, whether it is a peaceful approach, whether it is filled with anxiety, whether it is filled with difficulties or filled with apprehension, and so much more. This helps the medicine man or medicine woman who is facilitating the sweat lodge to uniquely provide personalized healing energy to each participant. Also, the medicine man or medicine woman observes the breath during various stages of the ceremony to be of better service to all participants. Whatever breath patterns the participants demonstrate, the medicine man or medicine woman will help them to transform the breath to an expansive breath which assists in the process of releasing trauma or constrictive images from the energy field of the person. The breath is a unique symbol of energy which resides within the body, mind, and spirit.

The following invocations can be used to acquire empowering futuristic skills that would be beneficial to your present life. I have included a sacred invocation to help incorporate futuristic breath cycles that will help promote empowering thoughts and activate good energies within the energy field. Please read it out loud; this can also be read at the office. Normally, I recommend that you read your invocations before bedtime, but you can read them during the day as well. The first sacred invocation will help develop the awareness needed to receive information from your guides and helpers.

Acquire the Breath of Wisdom and Awareness Invocation

By the power of my good merits, I invoke my virtuous higher self, my virtuous teachers in spirit, my divine helpers, holy medicine people, the angels and helpers of wisdom, the angels and helpers of awareness, and all the wonderful beings who assist me in virtuous ways. Please provide your virtuous mentorship, intervention, guidance, healing medicine, and virtuous resolution to the following situation.

Please provide me your empowering and virtuous guidance, wisdom, and mentorship to help me develop and utilize the breath of wisdom, the breath of mindfulness, and the breath of virtuous mindful awareness. Each day, help me to become aware of how I can become virtuously wiser and make wisdom-filled choices. Here and now and from this day forward, physically, mentally, emotionally, and at all other energy levels. In full faith, so be it now, thank you.

Acquire Future Skills Invocation

By the power of my good merits, I invoke my virtuous higher self, my virtuous teachers in spirit, my divine helpers, holy medicine people, the angels and helpers of virtuous wisdom, angels and helpers of helping to learn future skills, and all the wonderful beings who assist me in virtuous ways. Please provide your virtuous mentorship, intervention, guidance, healing medicine, and virtuous resolution to the following situation.

I am aware that in the future my breath will be more advanced with the wisdom of Sacred Balance and virtuously positive qualities.

I request that every time I go to sleep that I am virtuously mentored to fully integrate into this lifetime the breath of Sacred Balance and a virtuously positive thought process. For the purpose of activating more great opportunities in my life and also activating more of my good fortune into my energy field and lifetime, help me discover my sacred self, exploring my positive future self. I realize my life journey is a holy life where I have lots of wonderful options and all I must do is think about these options to see my sacred self filled with fresh new wonderful empowering wisdom. Mentor me on wisdom-filled conversation and elevated language to help me become a great leader of my own wonderful life journey. Mentor me to have virtuous insights and approachability factors that help me progress extremely well in my career and my spirituality. Virtuously mentor me to develop the appropriate relationship with money so I can have the Sacred Balance of saving money and creating financial gains so my family and I can have a good life of prosperity.

Mentor me on the wisdom of good health, physically, mentally, and at all other energy levels. Here and now and from this day forward. Thank you.

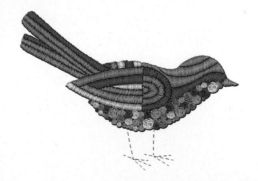

Invocations

SPIRITS, GHOSTS, AND ENERGY PORTALS

Energy portals exist for many different reasons. There are positive energy portals and there are harmful energy portals. Having said this, it's important to note that whether an energy portal is good or bad, one thing is for sure: the vibration and the energy of energy portals is very different from the energy within our space and time. Most of the energy portals I refer to within this book are harmful ones. Often people ask me: Why do spirits and ghosts inhabit places and houses? What is an energy portal and why do they exist? Why do spirits and ghosts use energy portals? Are there different types of energy portals? The mystical answer to these questions is yes, sometimes spirits and ghosts inhabit places and houses because, most often, they cannot find their way in the energy world. Therefore, they anchor to the places they know here on earth. What are energy portals? How do ghosts and spirits use energy portals? Most of the time ghosts and negative spirits use energy portals to travel to earth locations and not go into the light.

There are healing energy portals that our companion animals or pets use when their angels to come visit us. Also, energy portals

119

carry a tremendous amount of energy, very much like the swirling of the wind that can take your breath away or the whirling of the water in the powerful ocean.

Why do energy portals exist? There are times when energy portals develop as a result of an energetic change within that area, for example, when a calm neighbor moves out and another group of people who are violent, angry, and have drug addictions moves in. The shift of energy begins to be more evident day by day. This sudden change in the quality of the energy attracts a similar energy, which begins to affect the energy of the building and also the neighborhood.

Another well-known example of an energy portal is the Bermuda Triangle, where airplanes experienced getting lost. Those that returned reported seeing very old vintage airplanes flying alongside of them.

The harmful energy portals promote emotions such as depression, addiction, lack of vitality, sleep problems, nightmares, anger, negative thoughts, phobias. Harmful portals can also promote stagnant energy within the home and, interestingly, can also affect our prosperity.

Why do spirits or ghosts and/or entities reside within a energy portal? Sometimes when people experience an abrupt death, it is too overwhelming and the spirit of the person who died refuses to leave this world. They gravitate to the places they know and never want to leave these places and even work with harmful energy to maintain their space in time, kind of like fighting for their territory. Other times, unfortunately, entities manipulate the lost spirits and influence them to become like them and cause violence, depression, addictions, nightmares to the people who live around these energy portals.

The key element is to take control of this situation with a sacred invocation to call for assistance from angels and spirit helpers to shut down the portal and pick up all the entities to take them to receive healing, thus regaining peace within your home or office or region of land. It is important to know that you have dominion over the space. You have sovereignty over your home, office, and land. You and your family have the right to live peacefully in your home or office. The angels and divine helpers wish to provide healing, thus evolution, to all living systems and that includes entities and energy portals, so we all can step into the integrity of our divine light. It is the basic law of enlightenment and the law of evolution.

Through my fieldwork I have collected significant information regarding energy portals and solutions for the energy portals which are unsettling and harmful for our families.

Often, portals begin rather lightly with gentle energy activity but then as time progresses the energy starts getting frightening and more stressful. Some energy portals have sounds like a strange ringing in the area or flashes of light. Eventually, it starts becoming more intense and frightening. Also, during sleep time often, negative and unsettling images, sounds, and feelings felt by the people who live there. However, nothing is more powerful than our divine helpers and the Creator.

My personal experience can provide some great insights to these situations. However, before I begin, I would like to share an uplifting piece of wisdom about these types of circumstances. You and your wonderful family have the Creator's blessing of dominion over your living space. That means the Creator provided you authority over the energy around you. You preside over and reign over your living space and your energy field, whether it is within your home, office or even your mind, body, and energy field, which is sometimes called your aura. Wherever your body, mind, and spirit can take you—and this includes your dream time—you have dominion over the energy around you, especially if the energy is harmful, intrusive, damaging to your energy, your mind, body, and spirit. This also includes the energy around your loving family. You have energetic living rights to your home and wherever you spend your time. This is a universal principle and a mystical law and the minute we understand this universal principle we can virtuously and mindfully navigate your space and your energy field wisely.

Here is a insightful and useful personal story, that can illustrate this principle. Many moons ago a friend of mine invited me to a gathering which was taking place at her friend's house. I was very young at the time and still in training with my teachers. My friend said she was invited to a full moon ceremony. It was not a Native American full moon ceremony and my friend was very happy and excited I was coming with her to this gathering. I felt comfortable and agreed to accompany her, as I had asked my spirit guides days before if there would be any harmful energy at this gathering. They said, there was no harm at this gathering, so I said I would be happy to accompany her. I was a guest, and did not intend to facilitate any part of the full moon ceremony. We arrived, the door opened to a woman with a sweet smile. She smiled at me and said I was welcome and to come on in.

As I took one step into her kitchen all the cabinets immediately flung open, and all the pots and pans were shifting by themselves and were pressing up against the dishes and wall behind them. I saw the spirits that were in that kitchen immediately trying to hide from me by going into the kitchen cabinets, pressing into the pots and dishes in the cabinets. I thought, *Are these bad spirit or lost spirits; why are they afraid of me? Why are they trying to hide from me?* I heard my spirit guides and helpers say, "They see your light, it is as bright as the sun; in the energy world, your light represents a powerful energy. They are afraid and are hiding because they want to stay here in this house, but they also know that you have the capability to have angels take them home to the light."

I spoke with my guides with my internal voice: *But I am not here to facilitate ceremony. What is my purpose with these spirits who live in this house with these people? Are they good spirits, are they lost spirits, or are they supposed to be here?* My spirit guides said they were neither good nor bad; some of these spirits were ancestors of the people who live there, and some of the sprits were people who died there.

My spirit guides showed me for the first time a different type of energy portal which was active within this house, that allowed spirits and energy of all kinds to travel from the various realms of the spirit world to the house. My spirit guides said there are various types of energy portals. All this happened in just moments, as I stood there in the kitchen. The woman stood there in astonishment with her hand on her heart as if something took her breath away. I could hear her thoughts; she was bewildered and not sure what to say to me. I helped her close the kitchen cabinets and I saw the spirits that were hiding in the cabinets. These spirits were not sure what I would do. I sent them a mind message that I was not there to do a ceremony to take them to the light, but if they were doing harm in the house they would need go to the light for peace. I continued to help her close the cabinets, I sent healing energy to the woman of the house, and she quickly became comfortable and acted as if nothing bad happened. I let the incident go because I did not want to attract attention to myself.

We proceeded into a large living room where other guests were sitting comfortably on various sofas and chairs and talking amongst themselves. I was introduced to everyone, and I sat close to the windows. It was a warm clear summer evening, and the sun was setting. The group started with a short prayer, and I was quietly glancing over to the spirits of the house; they appeared to be a bit stressed as they glanced out the window. I followed their glance to something they were looking at outside of the house. I saw very clearly a spirit outside of the house and approximately ten feet away. This spirit had a harmful energy around it. The aura of this spirit was distorted and filled with brownish energy and malformed. This indicates non-virtuous energy. While the rest of the people seated in the living room were preoccupied with the full moon ceremony, I began assessing the energetic situation. I realized that the portal within the house was being used by all kinds of spirits and the spirits I met in the kitchen were very nice but the spirit that was outside waiting for me to leave was a non-virtuous entity. My teachers who trained me said when we clear a house of non-virtuous energies that we need to ask for our guides and inner plane helpers to pick up all non-virtuous energies and entities that have been around the house for the past seventy-two hours. We do this because spirits are very smart and can step outside of the house and wait until we clear the house and then when we leave, they come back into the house, but if we ask our inner plane helpers to pick up all non-virtuous energies and entities that have been around the house for the past seventy-two hours, it would not matter if these entities stepped outside while I was there. Our inner plane helpers would pick up all non-virtuous energies and entities that had been in the house for the past seventy-two hours no matter where they were.

The entity that was waiting outside was indeed harmful and I asked my helpers and a special team of angels called the medics to pick up this harmful entity and take it to receive medical care in the spiritual world and fill the void with divine light permanently. In seconds this entity was gone, but the question in my mind was *Shall I close the portal and if I do, would the nice spirits be stuck here in the house forever?* I went inward into my heart and asked my divine helpers what to do. They advised to shutting down the energy portal. When I did this there were several loud thunderous sounds as if it was going to rain. I knew these sounds were coming from the realm of spirit and angels which usually appear to secure the area with divine light, which was a very different energy than was there before, thus the sound of thunder was from such a shift of energy. After a few moments the house felt lighter and the quality of the energy within the home was filled with harmony and peace. I glanced over to the spirits that were in the house and they also appeared to be filled with peace. I realized they were previously afraid to use the portals because they feared they might become lost and never find the light of the Creator. However, when they saw the angels, they felt they could follow them to the divine light of the Creator and the only reason they stayed in the house was they could not be sure about the energy portal and where they would end up, so they kept themselves occupied by helping the families who lived in the house.

One by one they stepped into the portal and once they entered it there was a brilliant light which emanated the quality of comfort, peace, and a healing medicine energy. There were spheres of light on the other side of the portal which guided them into this beautiful light; the rays of light were like liquid sun which were filled with vitality. And then the portal closed, and I was back focusing on the people in the living room who were finishing up their ceremony and prayers.

After everyone finished with their personal prayers, they mentioned this full moon ceremony was one of the most interesting and heartfelt gatherings they had ever experienced. I am sure they felt a great lifting of energy, but I am also sure they did not know about the portals and about the spirits that were in this home and now with the Creator. As I walked to the kitchen to say goodbye to everyone, I glanced at the kitchen cabinets and remembered the spirits who were there just hours before.

The moral to this story is there are so many different types of energy portals, and I shared my insights about the ones I have experienced within this chapter. This will help you to either close them or transform them, especially if they affect your living space and family.

Enclosed is a sacred invocation to read out loud every day for a period of thirty days and then as needed, if necessary. You will notice within the invocation I ask to have divine helpers pick up all non-virtuous energies and entities that have affected the home for the past seventy-two hours. The reason for this is twofold. When we are clearing a home of any entity or non-virtuous force they can actually just step out of the house and even move their energy field across the street and come back after the house is cleared. But, if we ask for the divine helpers to pick up any entity or non-virtuous force that has been there for the past seventy-two hours and take them for healing in the energy world, it does not matter where they hide, as they will be picked up and taken to receive medicine for their healing process any place they hide.

I have noticed, at times, I would have to shut down these types of energy portals consecutively for thirty to sixty days to permanently close the energy portal. Usually these type of energy portals reoccur due to changes in the neighborhood or if influenced by a shift of energy within the region. But, they also can be affected by a family member who has developed some bad habits such as violence, or possibly a new neighbor who may be using negative energy which, in turn, affects your home. You will notice that within my energetic narrative I incorporated a small section that asks for anyone within a five hundred-foot circumference that may be encouraging this type of stressful energy to be provide virtuous guidance and healing to promote virtuous uplifting thoughts and virtuous activities and transform them into virtuous energy. I have found that promoting healing for people who might be contributing to this energy portal may need some deep healing as well. It is very much like a garden that has weeds; it is important to pull up the weeds but also to condition the soil to produce flowers and healthy herbs.

Another interesting factor regarding non-virtuous energy portals is seeing frightening images, which is common. I have the medics take the entities and the lost spirits to the light and provide healing medicine so everything and everyone is transformed into divine peace and wholeness. It's almost like the spirits that have gotten lost within the energy portal become overwhelmed by the entities around them and they can't seem to get to the Place of Light.

One of my clients started experiencing an energy portal in her bedroom and she spoke about the chandelier starting to shake and then entities would appear like zombies or people with guns; it was terribly frightening, and she started to sleep with the light on and became stressed before nighttime. While I was taking notes, I noticed the area where the chandelier appeared to start to shake was the launching point when things started to happen within the energy portal. So, I focused on what was happening around the chandelier and remembered something my teacher shared with me. He said, time and space can go forward in time and backward in time. So, within my sacred invocation I asked the medics which are special energy spirit helpers to go back in time when the entities appeared and pick up the entities and lost spirits that had anything to do with the shaking of the chandelier for the past couple of weeks and also pick up the source and origin of the energy portal and take them to receive medical care in the spirit world and never return to the house and family. Also, I asked them to fill the void from which they were removed with divine light. Basically, with this request, I had the medics go back in time and remove not only the negative energy, but also the entities and source and origin of the energy portal. I shut down the energy portal and then cleared the area by having the medics clear the area. Their specific purpose is to pick up all non-virtuous entities and lower vibration energy and take them to receive medical care in the energy world. As soon as I repeated the invocation, my client reported that her home was peaceful, and the energy portal was gone.

Please read the enclosed invocation out loud two to three times daily and before bedtime. It can be read within the home, but also can be read remotely, such as at the office. The more people who read it to support your efforts, the more powerful it becomes. You can read it additionally any time you feel you need it.

The additional recommendation is to do an energy clearing of everyone's aura. Clearing the energy of everyone that lives within the home is a very good idea. I also recommend clearing the energy field of all companion animals that live in the home. Smoke cleansing is my favorite way to clear my energy field and also my pets.

Invocation to Close a Non-Virtuous Energy Portal

By the power of my good merits, I invoke for my virtuous teachers in spirit, virtuous angels, the angels of time windows, divine helpers of energy portals, and all my wonderful helpers who assist me in virtuous ways. Please provide your powerful and virtuous intervention, healing medicine, mentoring, cleansing, clearing, transforming and resolution energy for the following situation.

Secure that all non-virtuous access points and energy portals be closed and halted within my home and in a five hundred-foot circumference around my home permanently. Secure that all spirits, non-virtuous energy, ghosts, and confused energy and entities that have utilized the energy portals in my home for the past seventy-two hours be picked up by the medics and picked up by special healing angels and taken to receive medical care in the spiritual world for the purpose of creating peace for all concerned. Secure that virtuous angels clear out my home of all energies and entities that have the potential to do harmful and/or stressful things within my home that have been within my home for the past seventy-two hour. Shut down all non-virtuous portals permanently and secure that all non-virtuous and mental illness beings be taken for healing in the spiritual world and never return to my home or anyone else's home. I have sovereignty over my home and in a five hundred-foot circumference around my home. I have living rights here and my sovereignty consists of divine light and virtuous energy.

By the power of my good merits, I invoke for all the people in this region in a five hundred-foot circumference to be virtuously mentored every single time they go to sleep and also when the rest, to transform all their thoughts, their actions, their feelings, their contemplations, or their insights to virtuous wisdom and also the divine virtues of compassion, understanding, patience, and a level of awareness to be respectful and honoring of people, plants, animals, and their environment, so their non-virtuous energy does not spill into my environment.

Here and now and from this day forward, physically, emotionally, and all other energies levels, for the purpose of creating and maintaining virtuous peace and divine light within my home and in a five hundred-foot circumference around my home permanently and for the life of my building. Here and now and from this day forward. In full faith, so be it now, thank you.

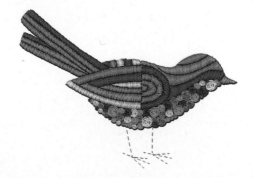

CONNECTING WITH AND
HEALING OUR PHYSICAL BODY

The miracle of the human body. Is it possible to regain our wellness? Given the right circumstance the physical body has the ability to repair itself, restore itself, and heal itself, and through the events of our illnesses we learn so much about how this can happen. In this chapter you will find a unique, useful, innovative approach to helping your body heal. In addition to establishing a deeper energetic connection between body, mind, and spirit through awareness and a powerful energy invocation, I believe the story I am about to share with you will promote a great awareness which can launch a deeper healing within you and change the way you interact with every aspect of who you are. It might be interesting and worthwhile to consider our vital and important relationship with one special aspect of ourselves, that helps us with good health and homeostasis. This special relationship is something that we normally do not even contemplate. The unique relationship I am speaking about is with our own physical body, and how our physical body relates to our sacred spirit within us and how body, mind, and spirit can work together on our journey which we call life. The most striking thing about this relationship is that our spirit needs our physical body to experience this wonderful life on Mother Earth in the physical form. Somewhere within our existence we lost our understanding of mindful wisdom-filled unity with our mind, body, and spirit.

As a provoking thought which will add value to establishing this important connection, I'd like to share my principle on wellness for the body, mind, and spirit. For me, it is not so much about treating an illness as it is treating the disharmony within the body, mind, and spirit. For when the body, mind, and spirit are out of balance and out of harmony, we will most certainly experience illness at some level.

As an example of the importance of becoming aware of the unity of our body, mind, and spirit, please consider the following concept. If you think about relationships in general, we would consider a relationship a bad one when the only time we spoke to our friend was when we were hungry, tired or needed to go to the bathroom. Or, if we spoke to our friend only during our neediest times and never entertained a sincere and thoughtful conversation, this would be a very unhealthy relationship. Also, if we continuously stressed a helpful supporting friend without so much as a thank-you and continued to do so until our friend was totally exhausted, this is, again, a very unhealthy relationship. Also, something as simple as forgetting to provide water to a hardworking friend who is working feverishly to help us is also abusive. This and so much more, we do to our physical body.

This reminds me of how we treat plants. Even though we cannot survive without plants, we often just use them and do not try to create a kinship with them. Plants have living spirit; they provide not only food for us, they provide medicine for us, they also provide spiritual tools for us, such as the Native American smudging ceremony. Thus, think about the relationship you have with your physical body.

Our physical body holds the same truth. We mature through the life lessons we experience with our body, physically, emotionally, mentally, and spiritually. Life happens and wisdom comes through those life lessons. But, somewhere down the line, we created the illusion that we are special and separate from all the other kingdoms on this wonderful Mother Earth, be it plant, animal, even our physical body. We even treat our physical body like a commodity, something to order around without so much as a thank-you or to provide it with what it needs to thrive and be in wellness, mostly through our unawareness. So it is not a surprise that our physical body demonstrates this unhealthy relationship with an illness. It is important to treat the illness, but, it is just as important to treat the core disharmony within the body, mind and spirit that truly facilitates lasting healing for any illness. Otherwise, the illness will return.

I'd like to share an important supporting story and then provide several energetic invocations within this chapter to help all of us, including our family members, to nourish and bring forward a wonderful new awareness and a deeper wholeness for every aspect of our mind, body, and spirit connection.

A woman came to see me, and she was very concerned and upset. She told me she had a pain in her lower back and had spoken with at least two medical doctors. After they reviewed her symptoms, they told her it was rheumatoid arthritis and provided her with pain medicine. The pain medicine did not relieve her pain. The doctors also recommended physical therapy, and this unfortunately did not relieve her pain. She was very worried; she could not get relief from any of these attempts. She asked her primary care physician for an MRI to secure more information regarding her pain and situation, but the doctor said it was not necessary.

She was confused and not sure what to do. I began by gently asking her a important question: What does your physical body have to say about all this?" She said, "Oh my God, I never knew I could ask my body what was wrong."

I gently smiled at her and said, "Well you have asked everyone you felt was an expert and it appears that they have not given you a resolution." She leaned toward me and said, "Do you think my body has that kind of wisdom?" I continued and said, "Our body will let us know when it is thirsty, our body will let us know when it is hungry, and even provides symptoms when it is out of homeostasis. It would be in our best interest to receive some wonderful wisdom, insight, and support from a part of us that truly cares and is the closest to the situation but also being affected by the situation—our physical body."

She became very quiet, and it was as if I had opened a door to a part of her mind that was sleeping and now awake. And so, we began a journey of healing.

I provided her with a special invocation on how to speak to her physical body. I have included this invocation for you or a family member. Through this invocation and a short meditation she found not only life-changing information, but launched a healthy relationship with her physical body. She also developed the courage to advocate for herself regarding her care and the healing process.

Everyone is unique; it takes time to hear what your body might be saying to you, especially when it comes to an illness or trauma. I would recommend trying to listen to your physical body like a friend who is helping you throughout the day. During the preliminary stages of connecting with our physical body in a mindful manner, it is important to ask if any activity you are undertaking, whether it is a thought or an action or an emotion is being done mindfully and with as much wisdom as you can bring to that moment. Everyone can benefit from having a better and healthier relationship with their physical body. Here is what she found out about her pain.

After using the invocation and a meditation she received a heartfelt conversation with her physical body. Her body showed her an image of a large cyst on the spine which was not only pressing on a nerve but also taking up space and her hip had started to be slightly out of place. Her body also showed her images of an event that launched this spinal trauma, but the most important part was she realized how hard she was on her physical body and decided to practice nurturing and wellness within all her physical undertakings. She also was persistent with her doctor, especially when her doctor said, "We normally do not do an MRI regarding your symptoms and your insurance probably will not cover it." To this, she said, "I appreciate your statement but please proceed with the MRI."

After the MRI was completed, her doctor reviewed the findings with her and said, "The medical narrative never mentioned any cysts or tumors." She was shocked and so surprised to hear this and went home very discouraged. She used the invocation again and meditation with her physical body and she received a strong message to secure a copy of the MRI on a disk from the hospital. So, she went to the hospital, requested a copy of the MRI, and took it home. She was so very nervous because she did not have any education on how to read an MRI, but she was determined to find out more information about her spine and lower back pain. She placed the disk into her computer and a thought came into her mind to invoke for help to find the information she needed on the MRI disk. So, she asked the universe and all her wonderful guides to help her find the information.

She loaded the disk and proceeded to click around until she got to a slide of her lower back and behold, there it was: a significantly large mass on the right side of her lower spine. She was so shocked and surprised; it was as if she could not believe her eyes. She quickly found her camera and took pictures. She immediately contacted her doctor's office. She brought the disk with her. The doctor began by asking her what was the urgent office visit. She pulled out the MRI disk and said, "Doctor, I know you said at our last session the medical notes did not mention anything about a cyst or tumor. I could not believe this so I looked at the MRI disk myself. Here is what I found." She then showed him the pictures of the large cyst on her spine within the MRI. His eyes became wide as he looked at the picture. He immediately got on his computer to look at the actual MRI. As he did so, he realized, not only was the cyst very physically present, but there were other smaller cysts around the area. He turned to her and said, "I read the medical narrative regarding your MRI and there was no mention of any cysts or tumors. You are a good advocate for yourself. I will speak to the radiologist and the reviewing doctor about your case."

The doctor did not apologize for this error, but the woman took the opportunity to convey that if she had not looked at the MRI herself, she would have accepted the information and continued without having the proper care to resolve her painful situation.

How many more people might not have received the proper care to resolve their medical situation as well? She also felt it was important to write a letter to the president of the hospital, which ended up changing the MRI protocol for all attending physicians to review the actual MRI in addition to the medical narrative of the radiologist. The universe also helped the doctors who were handling her case to develop better protocols which would benefit all other future cases.

This is a perfect example of how we cannot only receive wisdom-filled guidance by invoking for more information but learn how to be part of our own healthcare with wisdom and mindfulness. Had it not been for her wonderful relationship with her physical body, she would have continued with an unresolved medical issue.

In addition to the written sacred invocation, it is important to have a loving and respectful conversation with the physical body daily. This is very important to create a healing friendship and spirit connection with our physical body.

Here is a short guided technique to help you begin a beautiful conversation with your physical body. Please use this along with the sacred invocation within this chapter to have a better rapport with your physical body.

I always start out with a quiet moment to quiet my mind. I then close my eyes, take a few nice deep breaths, and settle my attention at the heart area. I then place my hands on my heart and focus on my physical body as I would focus on a dear loving friend. I then use the short narrative enclosed in the next paragraph. Here is the narrative.

To my dearest friend, my physical body. You have been by my side since the time of my birth. As I sit here quietly reaching out to you, I first wish to apologize. I apologize because I unintentionally did not realize I could speak with you. I unintentionally caused stress and also did not acknowledge you, honor you, and respect our relationship. I am sorry for ignoring you during all my undertakings and I am so sorry that I did not realize what I was doing. I also apologize for any harm I have done to you, in hopes that we help each other become healthy and stay in wellness.

From this day forward, I promise to have a loving relationship with you, and care for you in a mindful and wisdom-filled way. I will do my best to learn how to take good care of you and I hope you will forgive me for my unawareness and unintentional actions. Please help me by providing me some insights on how to heal all aspects of myself. Blessings to you, dear friend, and thank you for your wonderful presence in my life. Blessings to my dear friend who is always there to help support my journey. I am looking forward to your help and our wellness and our loving relationship. I decree to keep my body, mind and spirit in a healthy, wisdom-filled place as much as I can. I ask for you to help me by providing me with insight and I will educate myself on how I can be a healthier and happier person. In full faith, so be it now. Thank you.

There are also several invocations within this chapter covering the topics we reviewed.

The following invocation is to be read before sleep time every night. It is more powerful to read it out loud. Please continue reading the invocation until you see the results you are looking for or receive an epiphany about the stressful pattern.

I also recommend that you use a writing journal to keep some notes from the dream time. Our dream time is the world of more subtle realms of energy which help us work with constrictive patterns within our life's journey. Your energetic notes can be your most profound tools and provide not only a good progress report for all of the patterns you want to release but also help us to gain wonderful insights. I believe that journaling is where our true spirit and our ego personality can speak to each other and thus insights can occur.

Sacred Invocation for a Healthy and Healing Relationship with My Physical Body

By the power of my good merits, I invoke my virtuous divine helpers, my higher sacred self, my virtuous teachers in spirit, the healing angels of the physical body, my personal angels, my personal guides, and all the wonderful beings who assist me in virtuous ways. Please provide your virtuous guidance, virtuous wisdom, virtuous mentorship, virtuous intervention, healing energies, and virtuous resolution energy to the following situation.

Please help me to establish a healing relationship with my physical, emotional, mental, and spiritual self. Please help me to create a healing and wellness rapport with my physical body. Please help me to keep my physical body sacred and help me to have wisdom on how to heal my physical body and create good, healthy patterns that are wise and empowering. Physically, mentally, emotionally, mentally, and at all other energy levels. Here and now and from this day forward. In full faith, so be it now, thank you.

Sacred Invocation for Ailments within My Physical Body

By the power of my good merits, I invoke my virtuous teachers in spirit, my sacred wisdom self, divine helpers, my spirit guides, the angels and helpers that provide healing for the physical body, and all the wonderful beings who assist me in virtuous ways. Please provide your virtuous guidance, virtuous mentorship, healing energies, wisdom, intervention, and virtuous resolution energy to the following situation.

I have physical and emotional pain and I discovered (speak of you personal ailment here). I invoke for the wisdom on how to repair this ailment and knowledge on what can help this situation become better and healthier. This can include natural medicines and medical intervention.

Also, please secure virtuous wisdom-filled teachers in my sleep time to help me learn how to heal my physical body and also work on a daily basis to have good healthy habits to create and maintain good health for my physical body as well as all other aspects of myself.

I also invoke to become knowledgeable and wisdom-filled about how to have a better relationship with my physical body. Please provide me with great insights to help my physical body become healthier and happier at all energy levels. Here and now and from this day forward, physically, mentally, emotionally, and at all other levels. In full faith, so be it now, thank you.

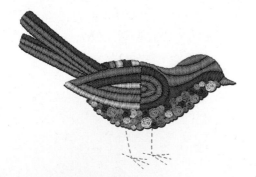

FORGIVENESS AND HEALING OUR MISTAKES

This chapter welcomes you to contemplate a deeper quality that is carried within the infrastructure of our mistakes. Also, how we can lift the spirit of our mistakes like the offering of a morning prayer to the energy world, for there is otherworldly potential for healing and wisdom. I share a story with you in the tradition of our ancestors to open the mind to the possibility that higher qualities of energy can indeed help our situations. I recommend reading the invocation at the end of the chapter every night until you feel lighter in your thoughts, emotions, and perspective about the situation that needs healing.

Mistakes are an energy in themselves that can teach us so many things. We all have made mistakes and the goal is to develop the ability of spirit awareness as to what our spirit is wanting us to learn. Through this awareness we develop sage-like energy, expertise, and ultimately a worldliness that encompasses the wisdom of the world and even the universe.

I know at times people feel so very uncomfortable when they make a mistake. Sometimes mistakes we make can cause a ripple effect which may include people judging us or causing us stress. At times we can be harsh on ourselves because of the mistakes we make. Most often, our mistakes involve others, and we feel sorrow for the harm that might have affected them. Oftentimes, we ponder and wonder if these mistakes can ever be healed. When I was growing up my teachers said mistakes are just practice and if we learn from our mistakes and strive to be a better person, the energy is lifted and we can experience a more enlightened life.

It is true that everything is energy first, and energy crosses the span of time and space. This energy principle is front and center when it comes to healing our mistakes and all the energy around what transpired respective to our mistakes. My teachers shared with me a beautiful concept regarding the universe. He said, "When we think about our past, it is no longer in our past but rather in the here and now." When we think about something that happened, we actually have summoned the energy of that event; it's like a time window where we can actually provide a healing vibration to that event, which means we can reshape and provide resolution energy to that event. When this occurs, we can also facilitate a beautiful turning point for all concerned including ourselves, thus healing the event and each and everyone within the event. There are many things that occur when we apply this energetic principle. Also, there are certain stages that can be experienced during the healing of our heartfelt mistakes, such as remorse, epiphanies, grieving, understanding, compassion, gratitude, and a re-awakening of what we would like to see as the outcome of our maturity.

The Great Spirit in wisdom and energy provided the wonderful tool of invocations, a great gift for all of us to use. I encourage you to use this energetic invocation to provide healing to any mistake you have made, which will bring it to a higher healing vibration. This will help you and all concerned feel the power of forgiveness, peace, wisdom, and healing. The first time you use this energetic narrative—also called a resolution invocation—you may notice the wonderful power of this invocation in several ways, such as feeling a great sense of peace and also a deeper understanding of the bigger picture regarding the event. I would suggest you keep a journal to record all your wonderful insights and possibly taking notes on any insights or downpouring of wisdom regarding your healing process. I also recommend you do some meditation and ask some basic questions regarding additional insights to help you and everyone concerned to heal from the situation. It is so very important to extract as much wisdom from the event as possible and that means doing a little meditation every day to ask what virtue and/or wisdom can be extracted from this situation. Again, please take notes because there may be many different pearls of wisdom and a variety of insights which help us to awaken ourselves.

I can remember numerous times when I made plenty of mistakes. One comes to mind when I was about ten years old and I invited a friend to an activity in town and completely forgot to invite my other close friend as well as an extended family member. Without thinking it through I hurt two people I cared about. One of them became so upset, she did not speak to me and started to send lots of angry energy toward me. I tried to apologize and she was still upset. I thought deeply about how my action hurt her feelings and felt her pain and disappointment. So I sat and wrote a wonderful resolution invocation and in a few days I actually felt the energy lifting from me and felt peaceful again. Within the invocation I also asked that my friend would allow me to explain myself and accept my apologies. A few days went by and then I happened to encounter her in my walk to school. I was so happy to have an opportunity to speak and possibly have a resolution. I began my conversation by firstly asking her to please accept my deepest apologies for my unmindful actions because I truly wasn't thinking and hoped we could be friends again.

She was quiet for a moment and replied, "I thought you were sending me a message that you wanted to end our friendship, but as I thought about it I realized it was a honest oversight and maybe I was being a bit too harsh. So I am glad we are talking."

I was so happy that she felt better and the sacred invocation truly helped us work things out in the energy world with our wonderful guides, thus allowing both of us to think things through and then have an opportunity to talk things out when both of us were peaceful and receptive.

Enclosed is a sacred invocation to use. The goal is to read the invocation below every night before you go to sleep. It can even be read throughout the day until the situation has been totally resolved.

Here is the sacred invocation to be read every night before sleep time.

Forgiveness and Healing My Mistakes Invocation

By the power of my good merits, I invoke for my virtuous teachers in spirit, my wonderful wisdom self, my personal virtuous helpers, the forgiveness angels, divine personal guides, my spirit helpers, and all the wonderful beings who assist us in virtuous ways. Please provide your wonderful intervention, virtuous mentoring, virtuous guidance, healing energy, virtuous wisdom, and resolution energy to the following request.

I have made a mistake that has caused some stressful energy in my life, and also has caused some stressful energy for other people's lives. (Place here the names of people who may need healing or peace as a result of mistake.) Please secure that everyone involved be brought to a place of peace, wholeness, and forgiveness. Halt all harmful energy to all concerned. Secure that honor, respect, wisdom, and peacefulness be evident within everyone regarding my request, harmoniously, instantly, and properly.

(Add this if there is harmfulness being projected to you because of this event.)

Please secure that the person and/or person(s) that were involved in my mistake (add their names here) be filled with compassion, understanding, and peacefulness with me. Keep them virtuously busy so they do not have time to even think about me. Also, halt any energy that is being projected to me or anyone else that is harmful and/or stressful and transform it to peace, here and now and from this day forward. Physically, mentally, emotionally, and at all other energy levels. In full faith, so be it now, thank you.

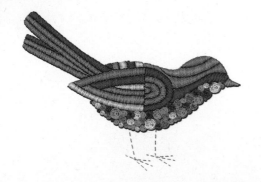

STRESSFUL PEOPLE WITHIN OUR LIVING SPACES

If you are looking for a way to transform the annoying people around you and, also, overhaul a stressful neighbor, everything you need to know about changing the energy around you is within the enclosed chapter and enclosed sacred invocation. Here is what is informative and what is useful in the energy world to brighten and enlighten those around us.

'This chapter shares a sacred invocation to bring about healing energies to our immediate and sacred living space, whether it is our home or our office. I am certain everyone would love a quiet, friendly, respectful, supportive neighbor, which can make life a little less stressful for us. Could it be that our neighbors represent a mystical symbol of something interesting that we need to transmute, not only within the stressful neighbor or annoying person in our life, but possibly, to a lesser degree, within us? Perhaps a symbol of unawareness or un-mindfulness within our neighbors is, surprisingly, also somewhere deep within ourselves. There is a mystical formula that is present within any stressful situation, including noisy and/or un-mindful neighbors. Here is the formula; please take some time to contemplate it.

It is not so much about the stress, but what the stress provokes within us that we need to focus and work on. When we want our neighbors to be more quiet or be more respectful of the community areas around us, we might find it interesting that they have a story to share with us as well. Which leads me to another mystical formula; all stressful events have, within the center point, one of three factors—bad communication, miscommunication, or no communication.

How do you start becoming aware of what was provoked within you? Simple, just ask yourself the question: what qualities and emotions are being provoked within myself? Whatever qualities and emotions are discovered through this process are clearly the blocks and obstacles to your power, your place of wisdom, and resolution to the current situation. If you have difficulties clarifying the qualities and emotions, I recommend you do a few meditations and asked to clearly understand the blocks and obstacles. My teacher said, you cannot change what you cannot see, this is so very true.

In this chapter the stressful situation is a noisy neighbor and it certainly gets your attention because it is disrupting the energy of your home and general well-being. One would have to assume the universe is trying to get your attention and a noisy neighbor is definitely not something you can ignore. This situation includes another great mystical principle which we can use to our benefit: where there is stress—there is focus; where there is focus, there is a great potential for resolution. A different way to see this formula is—when we learn all there is to learn from a situation, we will walk that path no more. Thus, the written sacred invocation will work on not only the noisy neighbor but also any and all that may be contributing to it.

The universe and the Creator also hold true to a principle called the *law of economy*, which states that when we call upon our energetic resources in the heavens, they come into this world to help us with the intention to assist in the promotion of self-awareness and the self-awareness of others into the situation, thus, evolution.

Here is a wisdom story to help support the written invocation.

I had a client come to see me because she was overwhelmed and angry with the new neighbors who shared a wall of her condo in her building. The new neighbors were loud, messy, played very loud music, and left trash in common areas. My client issued complaints to the building management about the garbage they would leave in the hall next to her door. She even called the police and reported them several times. Nothing changed and she was getting heavily stressed and very sick from all the stress. She complained that she was a wonderful person and demanded to know why this had happened to her. She was very angry, and yelling at the top of her voice at me in my office. She said she was mad at God and the universe for doing this to her.

After fifteen minutes of very loud complaining and emotional outbursts, I quietly said, "Send the right energy and the right energy will return." I mentioned everything is energy and asked her what type of energy she was sending to the situation at hand. I asked her, "What qualities of energy are you using to impact the environment and the situation?"

She became very quiet: She realized she was sending unaware energy and unmindful energy. I shared some wisdom with her so she could see this as an opportunity to resolve the situation. Before I began, I mentioned that I have a connecting wall to another office next door and I would appreciate if she would bring her voice to a softer level. She was surprised and said she always talks loud but she would speak softer to honor my request. As she began to speak softer, she realized she felt better speaking at a softer volume and she even commented how she felt more of her happiness come through. I told her that I wanted to be mindful and respectful of my neighbor who had an office next to mine and I appreciated her efforts to lower her voice. I provided an analogy to help her see that there is a great potential for transforming the energy and the situation. I said, "Let's look at this as a formula. You are point A and your neighbor is point B and in between point A and point B is energy. At this moment, what type of energy do you feel is in between point A and point B?" She was quiet and then said, "I am not sure."

On a piece of paper I drew the letter A and then drew a wavy line and then drew the letter B. The wavy line in between A and B represented the energy that was currently there. I then pointed out that the energy between point A and point B, in my opinion, would not be appropriate to produce peace and, just as important, would not produce the quality of awareness which leads to peace and coop- erative efforts. I repeated, "send the right energy and the right energy will return." She asked me to please help her understand what she needs to do.

I explained that it is a little like the old game of rock, paper, scis- sors. One energy is more powerful then the other energy and will prevail. The one force of energy that all aspects of energy will re- spond to is evolution. I told her it was clear that the neighbor was unaware of his own unawareness, but also there was a possibility the woman might be unaware of her own unawareness. I mentioned a personal mystical story that occurred when I was in a very busy re- tail store. I had my cart and was starting to head toward another section of the store when I notice many of the customers focusing on their phones and running into other people and products. They were so preoccupied with their phones and in a hurry, bumping into large shelving units and carts of equipment. I heard my wonderful guides say, be aware of other people's unawareness, but even more importantly, be aware of your own unawareness. I never forgot this

powerful wisdom-filled experience, a gentle reminder that unawareness can hold us in a place where there is no evolution, healing, and
resolution.

I provided my client a sacred invocation to place the appropriate energy in between point A and point B which was wisdom-filled
awareness. I asked her to not only do the sacred invocation but visualize an image of herself and her neighbor becoming more respectful
of each other and communicating appropriately. Then, to visually de-
posit the appropriate energy between them, which is virtuous awareness. By using the golden words *virtuous awareness* between them, we
could see many positive changes.

The sacred invocation worked and both of them became very
aware, communicative, and kind to each other. She also became aware
of how noisy she was and that she was playing loud music exactly like
he was. At the end of the story, she found out that he was frustrated
with her noise and was retaliating by being even more noisy. She
apologized and created a policy to call each other on the phone when
the noise was too loud. Here is the sacred invocation to transform the
energy.

Annoying and Stressful People Invocation

By the power of my good merits, I invoke for my virtuous higher
self, my virtuous teachers in spirit, my divine helpers, my personal
virtuous guides, the angels and helpers who promote mindfulness
and respect, the angels that transform unawareness in people, annoying people, and stressful neighbors, the angels that virtuously
mentor people who are not aware of their ignorance and transform
this ignorance to the quality of being considerate of other people,
places, and things, the angels that virtuously intervene to halt people
who play loud music and become very inconsiderate of others.

Please provide your virtuous intervention, virtuous mentoring, virtuous guidance, healing medicine, and resolution energy to the following situation.

My neighbors (name) are very loud, inconsiderate, not mindful, not sensitive to other people's needs, do not have community politeness, are not cooperative to learn, not willing to evolve, not willing to mature, carry very unaware consciousness, are messy, and do not take into consideration that other people surround them and that they should be aware of their actions, which should be honoring and mindful and not very self-serving.

Secure that my neighbors (names placed here) become considerate of their neighbors, become mature and have a willingness to do considerate good things, become very quiet and considerate neighbors, become conscious of their lack of community politeness, and proceed to have actions that are respectful and wisdom-filled. Secure they take initiative to become very active in community politeness. Secure all involved have a desire to evolve, be mindfully kind, virtuously self-aware, virtuously mature, clean up after themselves, keep the music and noise at an acceptable level for all neighbors, participate in kindness, facilitate peacefulness, and have the will to do good things. Please also apply this written invocation to myself and my family so we can become mindful, aware, and add positive value to our neighborhood energy.

Here and now and from this day forward, physically, emotionally, mentally, and at all other levels. In full faith, so be now, thank you.

Invocations

REMOVING HARMFUL ANCESTRAL INFLUENCES

In this chapter we will focus on removing ancestral forces that may be impinging upon our well-being, block us from our prosperity, or pose possible obstacles to our good health. We start by realizing that within our genes we have influences from our ancestors. Some of these influences are good but some are not so good. For example our ancestors might have been hunters and gatherers and we may have a tendency to move frequently from home to home. However, through our awareness, we have a choice and through that choice we lighten the load within our energy field and we begin to create mindfully, wisely, and produce an effect which can be very much like stepping out of a fog and seeing the true power of our existence and thus our happiness.

There are native Apache stories that tell of mystical energy in our DNA and genes. You might find it interesting that in the Apache tradition the genes and how they affect our daily activities translate into ghosts in our genes. That is correct, ghosts—traces or vestiges of energy imprints that may influence us, our decisions, our motivations, and even the way we negotiate. I am sure you have heard friends say, "Oh, he's got his grandfathers temper" or "Yes, our nephew has his mother's entrepreneur genes." Some of the native stories state that whatever our ancestors did and whatever our ancestors became through their activities can be imprinted into our genes. The genes within our physical body chemically guide our physical body to manifest the color of our eyes, the color of our hair, and can dictate proclivity factors for disease. But did you know that the subtle forces of our genes carry ethereal imprints that might provoke us to see life as a struggle? Or have a notion that money is bad? Or even increase our psychic abilities? Yes, the more subtle energy within our genes certainly exists within our DNA and is better known to the Apache people as ancestral forces, good and/or bad or maybe we should use terms, such as evolved and unevolved.

Our DNA genes carry the energetic blueprints of our personal life lesson that we have selected mindfully or emotionally for our life's journey. The Creator is very wise indeed. And here we are, born again on Mother Earth, a time traveler with ghosts in our DNA and a desired force of energy to walk this wonderful Mother Earth through our reincarnation process. Once again we recall the joy of feeling refreshed by a desert rain or recall the sweet smell of flowers and trees during previous lifetimes. Or even awaken a past life memory of helping a loved one in their hour of need, all to promote and provoke our evolution as a person and as an ancestor who has traveled this land many times before. As we walk this world we have our own personal deeds and pilgrimage, a quest to feed our spirit but also to resolve tendencies that are prompted by the ghosts in our DNA. There is a part of us that knows how important it is to lighten our energy field and fill it with wisdom instead of an automatic reaction from a past pattern. We take the lead in our pilgrimage to evolve and we are doing our best to cleanse and even remove harmful or lower vibrational energies from our genes, thus healing our ancestors as well as ourselves. But what are these ghosts in our DNA genes? They are energy imprints from our ancestors, specifically, the influences of what they have done in past lives and what they had become in previous lives. This energy anoints our genes with the subtle energies of certain emotional qualities, driving forces on why we do things, good or bad. These ancestral influences can help us or block us from evolving, but when we become aware of ancestral influences, we have more power over them. Here are some examples of ancestral influences. Possibly, an ancestral influence for power can cause depression. Sometimes, ancestral influence of greed may influence people to conquer other societies. Sometimes, the quality of anger or impatience causes a lot of open mindedness due to regret.

Our ancestral influences can also be helpful and empowering energy, such as the qualities of cooperation and helpfulness. Ancestral influences can also be the qualities of strength and courage, as well as spot-on intuition or accurate visions of seeing future outcomes. A good example is when we step into a memory of being comforted by the smell of a fire, the smell of sweet grass when it is burned before a prayer, or the way someone holds our hand when we need support. I remember when I was very young and stepped into my first sweat lodge. Native elders were singing their prayer songs and the fire pit was filled with the fragrance of sage and sweet grass. I remembered this place and the great comfort it had given me then and many lifetimes ago, because I felt I had been there before. An ancestral influence can be a driving force, such as saving every penny you have and having a rationale that saving every penny is not only important but is a matter of life or death. Where would you experience such a notion? Possibly, your ancestors provided that notion. Another example would be that your ancestors were intense warriors and in this lifetime you now have difficulties with the quality of cooperation. Of course, there are also wonderful wisdom-filled ancestral forces within our genes and we will most certainly want these types of genes to not only guide us but help us flourish.

We can also begin by understanding an ancient piece of wisdom we cannot change what we cannot see. Which means we must take time to think about the qualities and forces that move through us when we are under stress, challenged, and even when we have choices about what to do in any given situation. I like to use meditation or just a quiet moment to think about what emotions and thoughts move through me when I am making a decision or working with people and projects. If my emotions, thoughts, or judgments are less then wisdom-filled, I will place them within my invocation to remove harmful ancestral influences specific to those emotions, thoughts, actions, or judgments. It's very much like gene-targeted energy work to release us from the bondage of a force which blocks us from doing what is reasonable and what is wise.

Family Influences

There are also family influences which may affect how we cope with life. What is the difference between ancestral influences and a family influence?

An ancestral influence is a force of energy that is etched into our genes that may drive us to feel a certain way. A family influence is a force of energy that comes from our immediate surroundings such as a family member or a group of family members who expose us to their patterns and behaviors, thus potentially anchoring a habitual pattern that influences us with those behaviors and customs into our daily lives.

I will provide several examples of invocations that will remove harmful ancestral influences as well as family influences. This will help you cleanse negative influences and set you on a beautiful path of experiencing your authentic self.

I had a client named Josh whose father and mother were alcoholics and actively encouraged him to deal with his stress by drinking alcohol and using other mood-altering drugs. Josh realized he was creating patterns of using alcohol and other mood-altering drugs on a daily basis. He was so very fearful he would turn into his mother and father. He reached out to me in desperation to help him energetically remove these family influences. Since everything is energy, I agreed to help him.

My teacher shared that if a person had high self-esteem, they would never do harm to themselves or others. This is so very true. I applied this wisdom to Josh's written invocation to provide healing to his emotional traumas of the heart and additionally provided Josh the family influence invocation. Here's what happened.

The first time he read his invocation, he was in bed getting ready for sleep. He held his sacred invocation in front of him. His sacred invocation focused on his low self-esteem, lack of self-love, loneliness, as well as halting the family influences of alcohol consumption. As he read his sacred invocation out loud he saw sparkling lights in front of him; this also happens when I read my sacred invocations. He said he felt there were angels in the room. He also heard a sharp loud crackling sound like thunder outside his apartment. Josh said the sound felt like it came from another dimension or another world and he could not explain why he felt that way. He fell into a very deep sleep and when he woke up he notice he did not remember any aspect of his dreams, but felt lighter and very well-rested. He read the invocation every night and started remembering his dreams. The dreams felt to him like past life experiences and these past life experiences began to receive healing light during his dream time, which

Josh interpreted as resolution energies. Each time he had these past life dreams, they became more and more peaceful and had healing qualities within them. Each time he would rise in the morning, his thoughts and feelings were more about placing his energy into things that truly mattered to him, which was very new for him. He became aware he had choices and started to feel clear, lighter, peaceful, and his depression and alcoholic tendencies were disappearing. He felt the invocations broke the pattern of his family influences. He became very proficient at identifying behaviors that were not productive and still continues to work on other aspects of his life with invocations. I will provide this invocation for you at the end of this chapter.

The following anecdote is an example of ancestral influences blocking prosperity: I had a client that had difficulty with prosperity. I found there were ancestors who had taken an oath regarding money. Somehow his ancestors had the notion that money would block their spiritual growth. As soon as I removed this ancestral force, he was able to not only keep a job but was also able to save money for his prosperity.

As these ghosts in our DNA play out in our life journey, we choose actions and energy to handle them. The interesting part regarding the DNA is we can dismantle these ancestral forces and family influences, especially if they cause us to have lower vibrations of thoughts, emotions, and actions.

Following is the invocation you can read on a daily basis to help remove the family and ancestral influences which may be facilitating blocks and obstacles to happiness and wisdom.

Please read this invocation on a daily basis and often throughout the day. Please continue for at least three months. I recommend you periodically use this invocation throughout the year to secure clearing away the family and ancestral influences that may come up through your awareness.

Family and Ancestral Influences Affecting Our Personal Journey Invocation

By the power of my good merits, I invoke for the angels that remove harmful family influences and harmful ancestral influences from my energy field and every aspect of my being. I also invoke all my personal guides, the angelic medics, specialized angels that bring harmful ancestral influences and harmful family influences to a healing place, divine helpers, and all the wonderful beings who assist me in virtuous ways to assist me in my heartfelt request.

Remove from me harmful family and ancestral influences that may have come from my relatives and ancestors (place names of family members here if applicable), as it relates to my (place the problem here, such as anger issues, poverty issues, cancer, addictions, knee pain or lower back pain, relationship issues).

Remove these harmful influences from every part of my being and take them to receive medical care in the spiritual world, never to return to me or anyone else, permanently. Also, fill the void with divine peace, virtuous wisdom, virtuous thoughts, virtuous emotions, virtuous actions, and good health for me so that I can heal from (place here specific things or qualities you want healing for, such as judgment, my lower back pain, anger, bodily ailments, financial problem).

Also, I invoke the angels that remove past life traumas and imprints to remove these imprints and/or traumas from my energy field and also remove the source of origin off my energy field and every aspect of my being. Take them all to receive medical care in the spiritual world and totally transform into virtuous energy, never to return to me or anyone else.

Fill the void from which they were removed with divine light, virtuous wisdom, and good health for me. I readily accept this wonderful assistance and healing. Here and now and from this day forward, physically, emotionally, mentally, and at all other energy levels. In full faith, so be it now, thank you.

LEADERSHIP AND HIGHER SELF

It may come as a surprise to you, but what we say reflects the level of our current inner maturity. What I mean is, when we use the same clichés to communicate with others, we are actually creating a stagnation within our thought process, thus not allowing us to grow and evolve. All great leaders do their best to stray from the words within them which are old and customary, hence it is important to use language in a new light and use these pathways to advance, to become fresh, and to become wise. This chapter is about developing a connection with our higher self which can guide us in such a helpful and knowledgeable way, promoting powerful leadership skills that can help our families, our careers, and even our personal journey. There is a great peace as well as knowledge that can be found when we align ourselves with this part of our spirit.

Many moons ago my uncles and aunts would sit and share great stories about the Great Spirit. They spoke about a wonderful leader and how a few of the young braves would criticize his leadership skills and often said they could do a better job, even though they lacked not only the knowledge to be a excellent leader, but also did not appreciate a good leader. As I sat with my uncles and aunts to listen to this story, I realized that I also hear this from people at work who complain about the leadership within their department, mostly about their bosses and the decisions they make. I found it interesting that even though we have evolved since the era of cowboys and Indians, I still find my grandfather's wisdom so very true; we must walk in a man's moccasins for a few miles before making a judgment on his decisions. Often people criticize leadership without seeing how they size up to the leader's tasks at hand.

One day a young brave followed the chief and saw him sitting under a tree making a sacred prayer to the Creator. The chief continued his drum prayer ceremony. The chief humbled himself and asked the Creator and his spirit guides to help him be a better and wiser leader for his people. As the young brave watched from a distance, he saw a bright light in front of the chief, showing him images and explaining how one event can impact many people, and as we evolve and become more enlightened we realize how good leadership takes time and also how communication skills play a very important part within leadership.

We know that developing and maintaining our principles and virtues is very important; however, if we cannot communicate with wisdom, it is hard to inspire and guide in a good way. Having said this, even when we are working with our children, brothers, sisters, mother, father, friends, co-workers, boss, manager, and even our companion animals, it is vitally important to realize how much we impact them with our words, emotions, and our energy. This chapter is about developing our sacred leadership and communication skills to develop our awareness and our abilities, especially with the assistance of our higher self. During my training, my teacher shared this most valuable mystical piece of wisdom: Difficulties come from miscommunication, no communication, and bad communication.

Life would certainly be easier if we learned how to communicate in a manner that inspires others, provides valuable information, and creates a desire to learn and understand more, thus, helping all situations become a cooperative effort.

This chapter will provide an invocation to develop our sacred leadership and communication skills that can truly help us in all situations. When we develop them, we can provide important information to inspire and transform all manner of things within our life. This applies to situations such as team efforts, helping projects move wisely, and even asking for a raise or bonus at work. So many of us take for granted that we are communicating well, but there is always room for advancement.

Please use this invocation to develop excellent leadership and communication skills. You may notice your psychic abilities developing, as these are needed to receive important information from your spirit guides. It's a great side benefit to this invocation. Also, you will notice communication skills improving and even become aware when you are not communicating well.

Please read your invocation every night, out loud if possible. Always express gratitude when it's completed to encourage a deeper rapport with your spirit guides and divine helpers.

Develop Sacred Leadership and Communication Skills Invocation

By the power of my good merits, I invoke for the angels of excellent virtuous communication, the angels of sacred leadership, the angels of clarity of thoughts, the angels of virtuous cooperation, my divine helpers, my personal virtuous guides, and all the wonderful beings who assist me in virtuous and empowering ways. Please provide your virtuous intervention, virtuous guidance, mentorship, healing energies, and virtuous resolution energies to the following request.

Please secure that my leadership and communication skills are wisdom filled, clear, mindful, filled with virtuous awareness, wisdom-filled cooperation, thoughtfulness, virtuous team efforts, empowering inspiration, and sacred leadership, for the purpose of achieving mindful goals, tasks, projects, and requests. Here and now and from this day forward, physically, mentally, emotionally, and at all other energy levels. In full faith, so be it now, thank you.

HOLIDAYS WITH FAMILY

There is a mystical reason why we have family, and every family has a story to tell. Nevertheless, I am sure you will agree that sometimes family gatherings can be challenging, from struggles with siblings other relatives, to absent parents. The heart is always filled with a want and desire to be happy. Sometimes the holidays can be a little stressful, especially when family members don't see eye to eye. Many of my clients talk about how stressful a family gathering such as Christmas or Thanksgiving has been in the past. Arguments and even traumas that have been part of the family infrastructure can use a hefty dose of an energetic invocation. The invocation in this chapter provides our spirit a productive effort and purposeful feeling to use a sacred invocation where we can focus on everyone, actively honoring and respecting each other. The invocation will also infuse the time that is spent together with as much peace as possible.

Please read the invocation twice a day until you start your journey. The more time you have to read your invocation before your family visit, the more powerful the transformation. Also, express gratitude after the family gathering is over and you're on your way home from the family gathering.

If there is a family member that has always had differences with you, it is possible it may be unfinished business from one or more past lifetimes. Remember this past life situation is a spirit lesson. The wisdom that you learn from this situation is just as valuable as the actual situation itself. Either way, remember that the universe and our divine helpers can assist by bringing everything to its highest quality of energy. So when we ask for peace, harmony, and virtuous wisdom within this family gathering, our divine helpers will provide these qualities.

The fastest way of receiving assistance is to ask for insight for ourselves so we can evolve. We can also ask for the most harmful family member involved to be kept virtuously busy so they do not have time to give you or another one else any difficulties. You can add the following words below within your sacred invocation.

Secure that (say the person's name) be kept virtuously busy so (say the person's name again here) does not have any time to even think about giving me, or anyone else, a hard time. Here and now and from this day forward, physically, emotionally, and at all other energy levels. In full faith, so be it now. Thank you.

Please read this invocation a few months or as soon as possible before the family gathering to allow for the universe to help as much as possible.

The Holidays with Family Invocation

By the power of my good merits, I invoke for my divine helpers, virtuous teachers in spirit, my virtuous family members on the other side, the angels that provide families healing, the angelic medics who remove all harmful and stressful energies, our personal angels, and all the wonderful beings who assist us in virtuous ways, to provide their divine intervention, divine healing medicine, divine guidance, and divine and virtuous resolution energy to the following request.

Secure that all my family members respect, honor, and cherish time together. (List the names of family members here that are especially difficult.) Also, I ask that all family members put their differences aside so that we can all spend wonderful quality time together in harmony and peace.

Please mentor all family members, relatives, spouses, and in-laws during our sleep time to continue to become enlightened and soften our karmic situation together into virtuous wisdom here and now, and from this day forward, physically, mentally, emotionally, spiritually, and at all other energy levels. In full faith, so be it now, thank you.

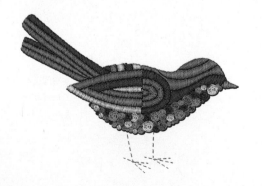

DIVORCE

Divorce is, symbolically, a transition energy platform. Divorce isn't an easy situation for anyone and mystically represents relationships of all kinds, especially the relationship with ourselves. This chapter provides well-defined energetic instructions and tools on how to clear the constrictive energy regarding divorce and replace it with new qualities of awareness, courage, maturity, and much more, achieving a fair, non-threatening healing transition of space and individuality. It gives ourselves the energetic freedom to grow in vast new spirited directions, healing ourselves and others.

I remember attending a wedding for a dear friend. As I approached the church there were large thunder clouds rolling in and starting to form darkness in the sky. These thunderclouds were filled with turbulence, thunder, water, and cold wind, especially, during the ceremony and continuing as we walked toward the celebration hall for dinner. A great wind and thunder ushered us into the dinner hall. There was a downpour of intense rain. I lightly glanced through a window at the dinner hall and viewed the bride and groom trying to maneuver through the strong wind and heavy rain. I could see the bride upset and complaining to him and the groom trying his best to create peace. The weather and that short glance were the energetic markings of their marriage and also the ending of their marriage a few years later.

In my native tradition, divorce is not a bad thing so long as we use evolved energies to help this transition process. There are many facets of the divorce process. Sometimes we are concerned about the financial aspect of divorce. Sometimes we are concerned about how the rest of our family and, if there are children involved, our children will perceive the divorce. Sometimes we are concerned about one spouse trying to leverage the family, and possibly children, against the other. A sacred invocation is very appropriate here, as everything is energy and our spirit guides will help everything be done in a peaceful, honoring, and evolving manner. That is their job to do; we just need to ask for their help.

I have written several sacred invocations to accommodate different divorce situations. Everything is energy first, and these invocations work wonderfully. The key is to read them every day until all the proceedings are completed. Keep in mind that you can add people's names, such as the attorneys, arbitrators, counselors, judges, in-laws and more into your invocation. Do your best to read your invocation right before bedtime.

I have also written invocations to help families find and utilize effective counseling services which prove to be most beneficial. Best wishes.

All Partners Receiving Help During Divorce Invocation

By the power of my good merits, I invoke for my higher self, my virtuous teachers in spirit, my personal virtuous guides, the angels and helpers of peaceful and fair divorce proceedings, the angels and helpers of the court system, the virtuous helpers that provide healing energy with divorce proceedings, and all the wonderful beings who assist me in virtuous ways. Please provide your virtuous intervention, virtuous mentorship, healing medicine, healing powers, and resolution energy for the following situation.

My partner and I are getting a divorce. I am concerned about our financial affairs, integrity issues, custody, and/or guardianship agreements. Also, that partner may not have been honest about many things regarding our relationship and finances.

Please secure there is peace around our divorce, myself, and all concerned. Secure all that is truthful will be revealed, instantly and properly. Secure the judge and all legal decision-makers use their wisdom to help this divorce be fair, peaceful, and wisdom-filled. Secure that I communicate in wisdom-filled ways. Secure that whatever I am supposed to learn from this situation is evident to me in loving ways so I can evolve and become happy in my life again. Secure that I represent myself wisely and mindfully in all legal decisions and legal matters. Secure that my pending ex-partner cannot send negative energy to me or any other part of our family. Secure that my emotional stress is transformed into virtuous wisdom for me. Secure that my in-laws are respectful and honoring to me and any other family members. Secure that I have a wonderful support system of family and friends that will help me see things peacefully and wisely. Keep all harmful energy away from our divorce and intervene at all levels to transform any and all harmfulness to peace, wisdom, compassion, and peaceful resolution for myself and all concerned. Here and now and from this day forward, physically, mentally, emotionally, and at all other energy levels. So be it and thank you.

Please add the following section if there are children:

Children Assistance During Divorce Invocation

By the power of my good merits, I invoke for my higher self, my virtuous teachers in spirit, my personal virtuous guides, the angels and helpers of peaceful and fair divorce proceedings, the virtuous helpers that provide healing energy with divorce proceedings, and all the wonderful beings who assist me in virtuous ways. Please provide your virtuous intervention, virtuous mentorship, healing medicine, wisdom, and resolution energy for the following situation.

My partner and I are getting a divorce, I feel I am very stressed. I do not want to be angry but it is so very hard not to be upset. I also feel I need to handle my stress better; please help me. I am concerned about our finances and all situations and family issues. Also, that my ex-partner may say things to our families that might turn them against me. Please help me with the following.

Secure that my children believe that I am a good person and any un-truths my ex-partner says will not change their love for me.

Secure that my ex-partner cannot send me harmful or stressful energy at all energy levels, and when my ex-partner attempts to send me harmful energy, that this energy will be transformed into virtuous wisdom for the purpose of allowing all of us to evolve in virtuous ways.

Secure that our divorce proceedings are peaceful and fair, as well as not financially draining for all concerned.

Secure that all my divine helpers work with my ex-partner to honor and respect me with truth and fairness during the divorce process.

Secure that anything my ex-partner says to our children be transformed into the quality of truth. Help me receive the wisdom regarding this situation so I can move forward with wisdom, evolution, and happiness.

Secure that my in-laws are respectful and honoring to me and my children. Secure that I have a wonderful support system of family and friends that will help me see things peacefully and wisely. Keep all harm away from our divorce and intervene at all levels to transform any and all harmfulness to peace, wisdom, compassion, and peaceful resolution. Also, help us find wonderful therapies that will help all of us be filled with wisdom, peace, and wellness. Secure that our children are treated with honor and respect by everyone, including both partners in our marriage, and that all custody issues be handled peacefully and fairly. Also, protect our children from trauma and stress during our divorce proceedings.

Here and now and from this day forward, physically, mentally, emotionally, and at all other energy levels. In full faith, so be it now, thank you.

REMOVING CLUTTER

Our immediate environment often reflects what is inside of us. Clutter represents many things and is perpetuated by unfounded beliefs and proclivities mostly from our past lives. Energetic stagnation and not being able to move into our productive self is the effect of clutter. Clutter speaks to our spirit for the need to vitally change into our self-awareness which can inevitably promote our self-mastery.

This chapter is about giving you an energetic plan of action to resolve the landscape of clutter as well as clearing blocked energy and understanding what clutter truly is. The universal principle, you cannot change what you cannot see holds true here.

Within the Apache tradition, we believe clutter stifles our life's journey and we begin to move this energy into a better place by invoking to become aware when clutter begins.

Also, clutter within our physical body equates to stagnation and congestion which does not allow for proper blood flow and circulation. This lack of circulation produces a deficiency of energy and reduction in proper use of our organs and systems. Therefore, the energetic invocations within this chapter will help identify the point of origin and resolution energy to clear the clutter tendencies at all levels. Medicine can come in many forms, techniques, and applications.

Within the Apache tradition, the term medicine has a great and deep meaning which launches a healing process and continues to assist us to become healed at all levels, experiencing insights, revelations and epiphanies, the lifting of constrictive energy from all aspects of our energy and mind.

Here is a personal story that can help demonstrate healing medicine. One of my clients, out of frustration, sent his wife to see me for an assessment of her life's journey and also to help her with many of the stress points that were currently happening in her life. Her eyes filled with tears and her face had the expression of great sadness. At home she always had unfinished projects and was squirreling things away even when she knew she did not need them anymore. Her husband was so frustrated because she started projects but had trouble finishing them, things were accumulating, stockpiling, collecting dust and endless clutter. She also had great difficulty with advocating for herself.

This brought great stress to her daily activities and she was so desperate to resolve this pattern. I decided to clear her energy field and energetically clear her home. I provided her with an energetic narrative to receive insight as to the point of origin and help resolve her physical and emotional clutter. I encouraged her to read it before bedtime. With tears in her eyes she shared with me that she probably would not follow through on reading the energetic narrative every night because she had difficulty following through with pretty much anything. I decided to have her read the energetic narrative in the office with me and then follow this with a short quiet meditation. We proceeded and at the end of our session something very interesting happened.

As she spoke with me she shared that her mind went to the dream world. She said during her dream time she saw herself in a previous lifetime. She was carrying clothes that belonged to other people, people who had more money then she did. The clothes were beautiful and surrounded her shoulders, her arms and legs. It was as if she was surrounded by clothes that belonged to very wealthy people. Even though the clothes did not belong to her, she felt somewhat comforted, protected, empowered, and safe. She said that in this dream she appeared to be very poor and worked for rich people and surrounding herself with their clothes somehow helped her feel rich. During parts of the dream she saw herself wishing she had more money and whenever she felt lost she would surround herself with her master's clothes. All of a sudden she had this wonderful look of freedom and amazement. She turned, smiled at me, and said, "Oh my goodness, now I know why I have all this clutter around me. The clutter comforts me, protects me, and makes me feel safe. Those patterns and feelings came from the past lifetime I saw in my meditation. It was like a dream but I saw it so very clearly."

I congratulated her for this wonderful wisdom-filled insight and encouraged her to ask her husband to read the invocation with her to help her follow through every night for a period of two to three months. She came to see me after a month, and she had great news. She started to clean up the basement and had more wonderful dreams about clearing more clutter in her home and office.

The following invocation is to be read before sleep time every night. It is more powerful to read out loud. Please continue reading the invocation until you see the results you are looking for or receive an epiphany about the stressful pattern. I also recommend that you use a writing journal to keep some notes from the dream time. Our dream time is the world of more subtle realms of energy which help us work with constrictive patterns within our life's journey here on Mother Earth. Keeping a journal is a great way of checking your progress. Your energetic notes can be your most profound tools and provide not only a good progress report for all of the patterns you want to release but also help us to gain wonderful insights. I believe that journaling is where our spirit and our personality can speak to each other and, thus, insights can occur.

Remove the Pattern of Clutter Invocation

By the power of my good merits, I invoke for my virtuous divine helpers, virtuous teachers in spirit, the angels and helpers of removing physical and emotional clutter, and all the wonderful beings who assist me in virtuous ways.

I have realized that I have a pattern of keeping clutter and clothing that is no longer of use to me. I also realized that I had a past life where wrapping myself with lots of clothing and clutter made me feel safe. Unfortunately, this past life imprint has developed my stressful habit of keeping clutter and tons of clothing around me, which has been stressful for myself and my family. I feel a loss of energy when I try to clear the clutter and get rid of the excess clothing. I wish to release myself of the proclivities of clutter and also buying and securing excess clothing and things.

Secure that my patterns, attachments, and emotions from other lifetimes and even from this lifetime that are related to buying or securing unnecessary things (and also keeping clutter around me and not being able to finish projects in a timely manner) be transformed into virtuous patience with myself, virtuous clearing of clutter both emotionally and physically, as well as virtuous time management. Secure that I have more than enough energy to clear the clutter. Also, that I take great comfort in the virtuous activities of keeping my personal space and living space clean, organized, and filled with divine love for myself and others. Secure that I do not find comfort in keeping clutter around and I do not find comfort in surrounding myself with clothes that need to be recycled or donated. Secure that I am not interested in keeping clutter. Physically, emotionally, mentally, spiritually, and at all other levels. Here and now and from this day forward. In full faith, so be it now, thank you.

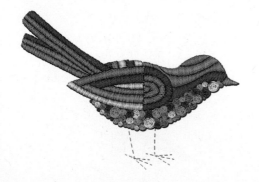

Invocations

REMOVING NEGATIVE THOUGHTS AND NEGATIVE ENERGY

From the earliest parts of our life, we understand the power and essence of thoughts and intentions. This is especially true during our upbringing, where we gain knowledge on how we feel when someone is not happy with us. Much of what goes on in our native ceremonies has to do with elevating our thoughts, which are the driving force of our sacred intentions, thus affecting our energy field and the energy field of others.

Within this chapter I provide the understanding of our aura which is also called mystical anatomy, and that we have sovereignty over our energy field and our life's journey. This chapter also includes an invocation that strengthen and cleanses our aura. The invocation and principles that follow will help keep your energy field clear of negative energy and negative intentions. This is especially important when there is depression, traumas, negative thinking, drug addictions, and many hardships. Whether they are self-made or the negative thoughts and intentions of others directed to us, when we apply the invocation within this chapter, we can promote healthy thoughts about ourselves and others, thus, promoting healthy vitality. This is our sovereign right. In the mystical books it is also called living rights within our energy field. This means that when someone projects a harmful energy toward us, or we are generally feeling unsettled we have the right to remove those energies off of our aura and the energy field of others.

Thoughts are energy carriers; this includes our own thoughts and the thoughts that other people have about us. Because all thoughts carry packets of energy, these energies can affect us emotionally, mentally, and at all other levels. While there is always some wisdom to be gained by any stress point in our lives, it is always good to see clearly at all levels. We can better navigate our energy without the harshness of negative thoughts and negative intentions. This chapter is certainly about how to clean the aura and promote vitality. When we clear our energy of harmful thoughts and harmful intentions we will feel lighter and think clearer; this helps us to be more in line with our great purpose and happiness.

The most sacred and powerful of all mysteries is the mindful direction of healing energy, which is part of this invocation. This is in addition to using the invocation within this chapter to keep your energy field clear of negativity and negative intentions. I recommend purchasing a small plant for your bedroom. As a medicine woman I love the plant kingdom. We intuitively understand that plants have the power to shift energy in a room or lift our spirit, not to mention help us sleep better. The use of plants and trees in our most important ceremonies is done with honor and respect, owing to the fact that we know they are the source of all our nourishment in body, mind, and spirit. Let the plant kingdom help you. Connect with your plant like a friend, which it most certainly is.

Please use this invocation whenever you feel your energy field needs clearing and cleaning of harmful and stressful energy. Please use this invocation when you feel agitated, worried, or any other distress that feels stressful. Also, if a number of calamities start occurring throughout your day or happening to another family member or friend, please use this invocation a few times a day until the energy clears.

We often do not know if there are any harmful energies from past lifetimes within our energy field. I always use this invocation if someone or a whole family has been experiencing multiple traumas, hardships and/or continuous accidents. Just as a point of interest, please try this sacred invocation and see how it can help things get better within your personal life and the lives of your family or friends.

Remove Negative Thoughts and Negative Energy Invocation

By the power of my good merits, I invoke for all my wonderful virtuous teachers in spirit, the virtuous helpers who remove harmful and stressful energy off of our energy field, the spirit helpers of peaceful and wisdom-filled energy, the angels and spirit helpers of safety and protection. The angels and spirit helpers who protect us from all levels of harmful energy, and all the virtuous beings who assist me in good and virtuous ways. Please provide healing medicine, virtuous resolution, guidance, divine intervention, and remove all harmful energy that has intentionally or unintentionally affected me and my family (imagine a picture of yourself and your family members or a friend in front of you).

Take all harmful energies and their origin off of myself and my family (or friend) and take them to receive medical care in the spiritual world, never to return. Fill the void from which they were removed with divine and virtuous love, divine and virtuous light and virtuous wellness, forgiveness, and wholeness for all concerned. Physically, emotionally, mentally, and at all other energy levels. Here and now and from this day forward.

Remove all intentional and unintentional curses off of myself and my family members (imagine yourself and your family members in your mind and also say their names or name of a friend). Take these curses and their origin and source to receive medical care in the entities world, never to return to anyone or anything, and fill the void with divine light, divine peace, divine and virtuous energy. Here and now and from this day forward, physically, mentally, emotionally, and at all other energy levels. Also, if there is any karmic debt, please secure its resolution gently and without harm in the energy world for all concerned to be at peace, wholeness, and forgiveness. In full faith, so be it now, thank you.

ENDING OVERINDULGENCE

There are many energetic reasons why we overindulge. A perfect example is the pattern of overeating. Whenever we feel stressed, we often do things that are not very empowering and not very helpful. The core issue is always energetic, and the good news is we can transmute and transform energy. Learning the energetic and mystical factors of overindulgence gives us more power over this behavior. However, the core driving force of all overindulgence is an inappropriate relationship we have with either eating, money, or whatever we are overindulging in. In this chapter, we will use the pattern of overeating as our example, but you can replace the word *overeating* with any other overindulgence. Examples could include an inappropriate relationship with money, an inappropriate relationship with people, struggles with time management, too much or too little exercise, and so forth. The example of overeating will apply to the invocation as well, and can be swapped out as needed.

The invocation within this chapter is very helpful in guiding you to shift from an inappropriate relationship with food to an appropriate one. My teacher always said that when we have an inappropriate relationship with something or someone, we will step into a repeated pattern of discomfort. Therefore, overindulgence is truly just an inappropriate relationship.

The goal of this practice is to have an appropriate relationship with all our relationships. These relationships could include nature, plants, Mother Earth, other people, other cultures, animals, etc. The relationship could also include how we interact with our habits, with money, with food, with self-care, but most importantly the relationship we have with ourself.

Here is a very helpful invocation to help you have the appropriate relationship with food. Remember, you can replace the word *food* with any other behavior you wish to provide healing. Please read this invocation before sleep time nightly, for a period of three months or more. Also, read this invocation out loud to add more power to it.

Ending Overindulgence Invocation

By the power of my good merits, I invoke for my divine helpers, the angels and helpers of dismantling overindulgence, the angels and helpers of helping me establish the appropriate relationship with food, my virtuous teachers in spirit, my virtuous ancestors in the spirit world, divine helpers who assist with traumas that relate to food, and all the wonderful beings who assist me in virtuous ways to provide their divine intervention, divine healing medicine, divine guidance, and divine and virtuous resolution energy to the following request, you are all called to aid me with this invocation.

I need help to have the appropriate relationship with food, so I stop overeating and stop eating unhealthy food and beverages. Please secure that my inappropriate relationship with food be provided healing medicine and transform my relationship with food to be empowering, filled with wellness energy, and virtuously filled with healthy wisdom-filled choices. Guide me to have an appropriate relationship with food and beverages and a virtuous sense of self. Guide me to the point of origin regarding my inappropriate relationship with food. Help provide me virtuous energy and gift me with the uplifting, empowering wisdom that will allow me to have a great sense of self and a wonderful great purpose. Guide me to create and maintain my healthy weight and to maintain my good health.

Guide me as I explore my sense of stress related to food and beverages. Please help to provide healing energy and transform it into virtuous wisdom and virtuous energies so I can be of virtuous service to myself and others through my empowering skills and uplifting talents. Guide me here and now and from this day forward, physically, mentally, emotionally, and at all other energy levels. In full faith, so be it now, thank you.

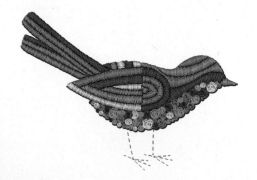

RESOLVING PAST LIFE ISSUES

There is a wonderful story in the native tradition on why we sleep. Many moons ago, the Creator made Mother Earth and placed us on this beautiful planet. The Creator said we had many lifetimes and experienced traumas during those lifetimes. The Creator gifted us the realm of sleep as a way of going into more subtle realms of energy to heal those lifetimes and also the traumas originating within those lifetimes.

Our physical bodies undergo maintenance and repair during our sleep time, but our consciousness does not require this. Our consciousness during sleep time will go into more subtle energies of existence, what we call *dreams*, and travel wherever it needs to go, past or present, to resolve trauma or auric stress points. In my native culture, I am honored and, in gratitude, have asked the Creator how to use this wonderful gift of sleep time to resolve trauma. The answer I received from the Creator was that they gave humans the power of words. I was given the wisdom that when you use words as medicine, they become medicine. The Great Spirit then designed a written invocation to help us during sleep time to travel with our spirit helpers to resolve these traumas. Why is this important? Because those traumas create patterns within our current lifetime that block us from our happiness and general wellness. As an example, this may be a pattern of not accepting our own goodness, which can block good things from our current lifetime.

This energetic invocation has been used for centuries to address difficulties in our lives. The following invocation helps our consciousness in sleep time seek out and transform blocks and obstacles that may have originated in a past life but most certainly affect this lifetime through a pattern or a belief. A good example of this is experiencing an aversion to cold weather and snow. This may be because, in a previous lifetime, we suffered from extreme cold and died in the snow.

Also, the Creator gifted us with dream time to connect with a part of our consciousness that helps us heal and develop insights and wisdom. I am sure you have heard people say "I will sleep on it and think differently about it tomorrow" or "I will go to sleep and feel better about it tomorrow." We all have this wonderful realm within our consciousness. There is a part of our consciousness that provides energy and wisdom to our dilemmas, past or present.

The Past Life Resolution Invocation within this chapter is meant to be read before sleep time with the addition of your personal list of stressful events, patterns, situations, or difficulties that are currently within your life's journey.

The Past Life Resolution Invocation directs that wonderful part of our consciousness to seek out and transform our constrictive energies from past and present lifetimes. A part of the Past Life Resolution Invocation contains a narrative that asks for our virtuous teachers, divine helpers, and angels to help us during our sleep time to transform these energies into virtuous energies for all concerned. It does not matter how intimidating a situation may appear because, as one of my teachers said, it's all energy and there is one purpose for all events and that purpose is to bring events to their highest vibration of virtue, self-awareness, and healing.

Many people have asked, how long they should practice the Past Life Resolution Invocation. I tell them to practice this invocation until the energy of their situation is transformed into virtuous energy. This virtuous energy will then release the practitioner and all people, events, and situations from the constrictive energy within our lives. Sometimes it takes six months or less, depending on the depths of the traumas within those past lifetimes and energy. However, even at the beginning of using the Past Life Resolution Invocation, you may feel an improvement of energy. The key is to be persistent and to do the Past Life Resolution Invocation every night until all the energy transforms into wisdom and healing energy. This resolution energy will, progressively, become an insightful epiphany or a level of awareness will develop regarding our stressful situations.

The meaning of past lives for native people, simply put, is that the universe uses situations within our lifetimes to help us grow and mature, to help us become self-aware, evolved, and become wiser. Past lives are a mechanism by which we become aware of our own unawareness and have compassion for it. They also guide us to become a more wisdom-filled person and to help others in wisdom-filled ways.

Enjoy the Past Life Resolution Invocation and keep a detailed journal of your dreams, insight, and healings so you can review them and gain more insight from them.

The following Past Life Resolution Invocation can be used on a nightly basis to help you to soften and transform points of stress, traumas, and difficulties that are happening in your life.

May you follow the integrity of your divine light and enjoy the help, support, and assistance of your personal angels, guides, and divine helpers.

This enclosed karma resolution narrative is to be read nightly with the list of concerns, whether they are physical, emotional, mental, financial, and/or spiritual. Please list them at the end of the invocation and continue to read the it until the listed items have been resolved. Some examples of traumas, proclivities, stress points, and patterns that may be affecting you in this lifetime could include smoking, drinking too much alcohol, other addictions, sleep problems, nightmares, low self-esteem, eating issues, traumas involving abusive family members, partners, or friends. Traumas may also include not being able to set good boundaries, stage fright, feeling fatigued, cancer issues, job issues, problems with bullies, and more.

The Past Life Resolution Invocation

By the power of my good merits, I invoke: divine peace, virtuous awareness, divine love, courage, good physical health, divine joy, contentment, serenity, gratitude, compassion, insight, nobleness, empowerment, forgiveness, a clear conscience, wisdom, strength, a gentle heart, a cheerful spirit, high self-esteem, intrinsic self-worth, clarity, and expansive organizational skills.

I ask to practice a wisdom-filled relationship between me and all sentient beings and to practice reverent communication with myself and others. I invoke all of these merits to support me, harmoniously and joyfully, in this lifetime. I focus upon the greater regard of my virtuous principles and operate from a great sense of prosperity and generosity in a wise and aware manner.

I ask to transmute my unaware and aware constrictive patterns and proclivities to these empowering substances in this lifetime. Please aid me in transforming the notion of struggle into mindful expansive, purposeful, and joyfully placed effort, which also facilitates spiritual fulfillment, financial success, and wellness at all levels: physically, emotionally, and mentally. I honor and send my gratitude to all my divine helpers and my spiritual teachers who provide me with this bridge of assistance. With deep gratitude, may all my helpers and spiritual teachers be blessed with wisdom and all other virtues harmoniously and joyfully in this lifetime.

During my sleep and dream time, I will work to harmoniously and joyfully transform, modify, and dissolve the listed past life traumas, proclivities, and patterns with the assistance, guidance, protection, and intervention of my virtuous helpers and teachers. Please provide healing medicine to all, thus bringing all to wholeness.

I decline the listed past life traumas and proclivities in the physical and the emotional plane. I cut the cord between me and these past life traumas and transform them into a virtuous substance for all concerned. I invoke my need to empower all with the divine virtues of awareness, compassion, serenity, high self-esteem, courage, divine peace, and divine love, all harmoniously and joyfully done. I decree that only virtuous transforming energy shall flow through me at all times.

I invoke to release myself of the bondage of the following listed past life traumas, proclivities, and patterns. I further decree to harmoniously and joyfully evaporate and dissolve the following past life traumas, proclivities, and patterns between me and (use this area to list out the traumas, proclivities, stress points, and patterns which are affecting you in this lifetime). In full faith, so be it now, thank you.

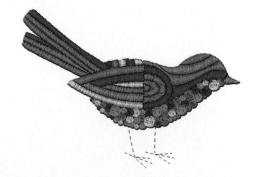

CONCLUSION

This book and the journey you are undertaking of indigenous ancient wisdom will provide infinite possibilities for resolution to your stress and the blocks and obstacles encountered each and every day. The hope is that you will develop a more peaceful and happy life, the possibility of enlightenment, and a wonderful partnership with wisdom-filled spirit helpers.

I have great confidence in the wisdom and techniques within this book and I also have great confidence in you and your earnest efforts. Never give up learning and applying your wisdom and techniques gained from this book. As you progress and utilize the tools within this book, your ability to see the bigger picture of your life's journey will be more and more evident and empowering.

One of my sacred intentions is to help you use energy to make a better life for yourself and your loved ones. If we all lived lives guided by our wisdom, enlightenment, and our spirit guides, how wonderful our lives and the world would be.

Throughout the history of the human kingdom, we have all sought a better way to live through connecting to a greater source of wisdom that is beyond ourselves. I trust this book of sacred wisdom will help you to enrich and enhance your life and those of others.